The Scientific Enterprise & Christian Faith

MALCOLM A. JEEVES

Inter-Varsity Press
Downers Grove, Illinois 60515

© 1969 by The Tyndale Press, England
Second American printing, February 1971, by
Inter-Varsity Press with permission from
Inter-Varsity Fellowship, London
All rights reserved

Inter-Varsity Press is the book publishing
division of Inter-Varsity Christian Fellowship.

ISBN 0-87784-634-0
Library of Congress Catalog Card Number: 74-93034

Printed in the United States of America

CONTENTS

PREFACE

In August 1965 thirty-six scientists from ten countries spent a week together in Oxford, England, discussing science and Christian belief. In this book I have attempted to expound some of the major conference themes, basing what I have written upon papers prepared for the conference and discussions during our week together.

It is with pleasure that I acknowledge the especial help I have received from Dr O. R. Barclay, Professor R. L. F. Boyd and Professor D. M. MacKay. Each commented on a draft outline of the present book and later read and criticized the full version before publication. At the time of the conference the participants gave me permission to utilize material in their pre-circulated papers and where this seemed appropriate I have availed myself of their offer. The names of the conference participants are listed in an Appendix at the end of the book and I have indicated in the text where I have drawn upon their papers.

One of the major challenges in writing a book such as this is how to communicate effectively with both the non-scientist and the scientist. Nevertheless the attempt to do this had to be made if one of the principal aims of the book was to be achieved, namely to set down with supporting arguments why we believe that science is a true friend of biblical faith and not, as is often assumed, in conflict with it. While all Christians must be conscious of the impact of science on their daily lives and faith, there are two particular groups who are probably more consistently aware of this impact than others: first, thoughtful students reading for a first degree or engaged in post-graduate research in science, and second, leaders of Christian groups, themselves often non-scientists. Ministers of local churches, for example, are increasingly, and at times embarrassingly, conscious of their lack of familiarity with basic scientific ideas. One result is that young people in their congregations at times pose problems which they cannot understand, let alone begin to answer. Such a leader may then seek to cope with specific issues arising at contact points between particular religious beliefs and specific scientific discoveries, either on a purely *ad hoc* basis, or within a framework which at times conceals an inadequate evaluation of either the biblical view of nature, or of the scientific enterprise and the knowledge to which it gives rise, or of both.

Since one of the aims in writing this book is to help such people, the first half is devoted to developing a biblical view of the relation of God to His creation, and a proper evaluation of science and the knowledge to which it gives rise. The second half is an exposition of some of the key concepts in modern science and their relation to Christian beliefs. The first chapter seeks to give a brief historical perspective to what follows. We have identified the two major protagonists who have conflicted from time to time as rationalism and rational empiricism, rather than science and faith. After developing a biblical view of the relation of God to nature, and of some implications of such a view for things like miracles, and the meaning of laws of nature, we examine the scientific enterprise, the knowledge to which it gives rise and the relation of this to other kinds of knowledge. We then ask how we should properly relate the explanations, models, images and thought-forms of science to those others which occur in religious thinking and writing. This leads on to a discussion of some of the traditional, so-called conflicts between science and faith. Here we examine the impact of theories concerning cosmology, evolution and the origin of life upon Christian belief, as well as problems of determinism as they present themselves in psychology, sociology and cybernetics. We close with a brief statement of the importance, for Christian scientists in particular and for mankind in general, of a Christian assessment of the practice of science and of the use to be made of the scientific knowledge to which it gives rise.

CHAPTER I

HEBREW-CHRISTIAN AND GREEK INFLUENCES ON THE RISE OF MODERN SCIENCE

WHY did the Greeks, with all their magnificent intellectual and cultural achievements, fail to initiate and sustain the rise of science 2,000 years ago? Why did the scientific revolution begin in earnest in the sixteenth century and flourish from then onwards? Was its rise in any way dependent upon, or otherwise related to, that other re-awakening which began in the sixteenth century, namely the religious re-awakening? Although a brief discussion of such complex questions has all the dangers of over-simplification, we believe we must try to outline some of the main answers at the start of a book like this.

In the centuries immediately preceding the sixteenth, an attitude towards the natural world began to crystallize out, which was to set the stage for the emergence of modern science. In his conference paper Schweitzer pointed out that, of the diverse influences which contributed to this attitude, two major ones can be detected : the influence of Greek thinking and the influence of Hebrew-Christian thinking. These two streams of thought, which had flowed together many centuries before, had inevitably interacted in numerous ways, producing alterations in each. By examining these two streams and some of their interactions, we may be able to focus upon the salient features of those attitudes towards nature which were to be so essential to the rise and development of modern science, as well as on those which may have delayed its beginning and constitute a threat to its continuation and development.

Hooykaas cautioned that to speak of a Greek view of nature is, of course, somewhat misleading, in that it fails to do justice to the wide spectrum of views which we now know were held by Greek thinkers in the six centuries up to the third century before Christ. Even so we can detect certain aspects of the Greek views of nature which seem to run as a common theme through most of them, and which have had an enduring influence on all later western thought on this subject.

Let us consider some of these, following the outline of Schweitzer's conference paper. Greek thinkers firmly held that the universe should be regarded as non-created and therefore as existing from eternity to eternity. Since it was eternal, it was also divine or semi-divine. Guthrie puts it thus : 'The most noteworthy believer in the eternity of the universe was, of course, Aristotle, and he makes frequent mention of the cyclic theory of human affairs. . . . But it occurs in his master Plato, and also in later writers like Polybius and Lucretius.'[1] As Guthrie points out when discussing Anaximander's view as described by Aristotle, 'The same mysterious x which is what we might call the material sub stratum of the world, is also the force which guides or directs it. It is not only everlasting, but everlastingly alive, immortal and divine.'[2]

Not only was the universe regarded as divine, but as a consequence of this the Greeks considered also that the world was being moved in a purposeful way by indwelling divine forms. Guthrie, while acknowledging that our knowledge of the early Greek philosophers is sadly circumscribed by the fact that their own writings have perished, adds that 'there is no need for scepticism, however, when we read that Anaximenes thought of the air as God, and also drew an analogy between the air which sustains the universe and the human soul. The idea that the whole world is a living and breathing creature was firmly upheld by the Pythagoreans and finds its most striking expression in Timaeus. . . . Thus everything is made of one substance, and that substance, at least in its most properly balanced, invisible form, is the substance of life. Since it is everlastingly alive, it is divine, for immortality and divinity were two inseparable concepts for a Greek. The

[1] W. K. C. Guthrie, *In the Beginning* (Methuen, 1957), p. 65.
[2] W. K. C. Guthrie, *op. cit.,* p. 48.

life principle in finite creatures is the same. Perhaps that is what Thales meant in one of the few sayings which can be plausibly assigned to him : "everything is full of Gods".[3]

This indwelling of nature by divine forms provided an immediate link between man and nature, since the mind of man was also believed to possess the same divine character attributed to the forms of nature. Such a belief, however, does not go unchallenged, as Guthrie reminds us when he points out that Theophrastus's doctrine, 'the air within us is a small portion of the God', was parodied by Aristophanes, 'when in one of his comedies he brings Socrates onto the stage suspended in the air in a basket. Asked the reason for this strange proceeding, Socrates replied that to discover the truth about celestial matters, he must allow his mind to mingle with the kindred air.'[4]

Even so, since both the mind of man and the forms of nature were alike divine, it was assumed that the one could read off or intuit the other. And, of course, since for the Greek reason was the principal tool of the mind of man, it was reason that would be the key to the mysteries of nature. It was the firm belief in reason which was the corner-stone of Greek speculation about the origin and nature of the universe. As Kitto reminds us, 'Here we meet a permanent feature of Greek thought : the universe, both the physical and the moral universe, must be not only rational, and therefore knowable, but also simple.'[5] So great was this belief in reason that, he (the Greek) 'tended to impose pattern where it was in fact not to be found, just as he relied on reason where he would have been better advised to use observation and deduction'.[6]

It is just at this point that we begin to glimpse ways in which the tremendous achievements of the Greeks in the development of logical reasoning were in danger of becoming the very factors which were to place limits on the development of empirical science. As Sambursky sums it up in *The Physical World of the Greeks*, 'The ancient Greek believed fundamentally that the world should be *understood,* but that there was no need to *change* it. This remained the belief of subsequent generations up to the Renaissance. This passive attitude to the practical use of the forces

[3] *Ibid.*, p. 49.
[4] *Ibid.*, p. 50.
[5] H. F. D. Kitto, *The Greeks* (Penguin Books, 1951), p. 179.
[6] *Ibid.*, p. 187.

of nature was reinforced by the complete ossification of the natural science in the Middle Ages in the condition to which Aristotle had brought them.'[7] And, as G. S. Kirk concurs in his review of Sambursky's book in the *Classical Review,* 'In modern science there is a balanced use of induction and deduction; theory and practical application help one another. The Greeks, on the other hand . . . formed a priori hypotheses too readily, and neglected close and systematic observation and experiment—largely because their main motive, as Aristotle approvingly said, was curiosity, rather than the attempt to dominate nature.'[8]

We thus see that the magnificent intellectual achievements of the Greeks, which were destined to rule over western thought for two millennia, had limitations inherent in them which were to prevent them from bringing forth modern science, unaided by other streams of thought. There were probably three features of Greek thought which most consistently inhibited the development of a modern scientific approach. In the first place there was not felt any necessity for empirical testing, for, as Sambursky put it in the quotation cited above, 'The ancient Greek believed fundamentally that the world should be *understood,* but that there was no need to *change* it.' There was no necessity to stoop to handle the world in order to understand it; contemplation allied to reasoning was sufficient. Secondly, since the Greek view of nature regarded the universe and the various parts thereof to be indwelt by living forms, usually divine in character, it was perfectly natural to look for teleological explanations to the exclusion of other types. And thirdly, because the mind of man was rational, the Greek elevated the processes of intuition and the use of reason above careful observation. As Guthrie puts it, while quoting Daremburg with approval, ' . . . the philosophers tried to explain nature while shutting their eyes'.[9]

For all these shortcomings there were other features of Greek thinking which constituted the germinal seeds for the eventual development of modern science. In the first place the world *did* have order in spite of the apparent chaos, as Kitto says: 'The

---

[7] S. Sambursky, *The Physical World of the Greeks* (Routledge and Kegan Paul, 1963), p. 230.
[8] G. S. Kirk, 'Review of *The Physical World of the Greeks*' in the *Classical Review,* Vol. VIII, No. 2, June 1958, pp. 111-116 (quotation from p. 111).
[9] W. K. C Guthrie, *Greek Philosophy* (CUP, 1953), p. 190.

Greek never doubted for a moment that the universe is not capricious : it obeys Law and is therefore capable of explanation.'[1] Secondly, they saw clearly the worth of a body of knowledge about nature. Thirdly, they discovered and perfected a method of deductive reasoning. Fourthly, they produced some remarkable developments in philosophy, logic and mathematics, all of which were to be basic and essential tools for the eventual rapid development of science. So that just as 'their eyeshutting retarded the growth of science', so 'their mind opening led to things perhaps equally important, metaphysics and mathematics'. And finally, they made significant beginnings in astronomy, physics and biology.

Even so it now seems clear that just as scientific progress was given its initial impetus by the Greeks, so it was eventually inhibited by the same a priori attitude which gave it its initial stimulus. Thus a highly developed system of deductive reasoning could soon have a stifling effect and inhibit new discovery unless the initial presuppositions to which such reasoning was applied were themselves subject to criticism in the light of careful observation and experiment. In due course we can see the slow penetration of ideas coming from other traditions, notably the Hebrew-Christian tradition, and it is to these that we must now turn.

Chronologically, of course, the Old Testament comes before the intellectual age of the Ancient Orient and Greece. It was with the rediscovery of the Bible and of its message at the time of the Reformation, however, that a new impetus came to the development of science. This new impetus, flowing together with all that was best in Greek thinking, was to produce the right mixture to detonate the chain reaction leading to the explosion of knowledge which began at the start of the scientific revolution in the sixteenth century, and which is proceeding with ever-increasing momentum today.

THE HEBREW-CHRISTIAN VIEW OF NATURE

What are the salient features of the Hebrew-Christian view of nature? The most outstanding one is that of a world totally dependent upon God. Let us consider some implications of this. By contrast with the Greek view, we find that the world is non-

[1] H. F. D. Kitto, op. cit., p. 176.

eternal, that it is created by God (Gn. 1) and is dependent upon Him for its continuing moment-by-moment existence (Heb. 1 : 3). God and nature are not to be identified with each other; they are rather to be sharply separated. God is eternal, and nature is created and will one day pass away. As the psalmist puts it (Ps. 102 : 25–28), 'Of old thou didst lay the foundation of the earth, and the heavens are the work of thy hands. They will perish, but thou dost endure; they will all wear out like a garment. Thou changest them like raiment, and they pass away; but thou art the same, and thy years have no end.'

Secondly, the natural order is not divine; it is created. *God* made the firmament (Gn. 1 : 7); it is an ordered world but not an autonomous one. 'Thou hast made the moon to mark the seasons; the sun knows its time for setting. Thou makest darkness, and it is night' (Ps. 104 : 19,20). The createdness of the world is emphasized at the opening of John's Gospel, for 'all things were *made* through him, and without him was not anything made that was made'. Not only did God take the initiative in creating the world, but the world continues to be only by reason of His sustaining activity in 'upholding all things by his word of power', as the writer to the Hebrews puts it, writing of the work of Christ (Heb. 1 : 3). Whereas for the Greek the workings of nature were rationalistic and purposive, with the purposefulness firmly embedded within nature itself, in the Hebrew-Christian tradition purpose resides in God, not in nature. If man wishes to discover the patterns of order in nature he must have recourse to experience, for he cannot discover them by intuition or reason alone.

For the Hebrew, God alone is to be worshipped; nature is only His creation and to worship that is idolatry—and he knew that the Lord God would have no idolatry. As Deuteronomy 6 : 4 teaches, 'The Lord our God is one Lord.' Nature was for him a gift of God to be used. As we read in Genesis 1 : 28, we are to 'fill the earth and subdue it'; we are to 'have dominion over' it. And finally, since the mind of man like the rest of him is part of the created order, it is thus non-divine and subject to error, and it cannot infallibly intuit or read off from nature the inherent qualities of nature. In any case, there are limits to man's intellectual achievement since God's thoughts are higher than man's thoughts (*cf.* Is. 55 : 8). With this very brief review of the salient features of the Greek and Hebrew-Christian attitudes towards nature in mind, let us now sketch their interaction and examine its importance for the rise of science.

Before the seventeenth century there were, from time to time, brief episodes when these two streams interacted, notably from the eleventh century onwards, when Aristotelian natural philosophy was introduced into the West, and Thomas Aquinas made his brilliant synthesis of this with Christian thought. We thus find scholastic thought based upon both reason and revelation, and showing a synthesis of elements of Greek philosophy and biblical faith. For Aquinas the crucial feature of all events in the world was their contingency. They might not have occurred, but they did. Certainly Aquinas portrays God not just as the original Creator, but as the One who continues to rule over nature and to sustain it from moment to moment. At the same time he accepted many of the deductions from Aristotelian philosophy, such as that it was a priori impossible that natural compounds could be made by man, and that it was impossible that heavenly bodies should have any motion except perfectly circular ones. He was certainly eager to defend the miraculous, and in fact encouraged the study of nature (in Aristotelian terms), so that miracles might not be ascribed to other causes. According to Aquinas's view, the knowledge of natural things would better enable us to recognize supernatural events. This sharp distinction between natural and supernatural events was to loom large in much subsequent Christian thought, both Roman Catholic and Protestant, as we shall see later.

This view, however, did not go unchallenged, as Hooykaas points out: 'The Bishop of Paris (Etienne Tempier) in 1277 condemned all theses that submitted God's incomprehensible will to human reason and, consequently, he admitted all the possibilities which had been excluded by Aristotelian philosophy, since he held that man cannot decide beforehand what it pleases God to perform in nature.'[2]

And this protest against Greek and scholastic rationalism was maintained in the next century when the Nominalist philosophers asserted that nature should be accepted as readily when it transcends, or seems to contradict, human reason as when it does not.

[2] R. Hooykaas, *Philosophia Libera: Christian Faith and the Freedom of Science* (Tyndale Press, 1957), p. 16.

As Hooykaas says, 'Precisely because they discarded rationalistic pretensions, the Nominalists could tackle scientific problems in a rational way; their reason was not their god; it was used to criticize rather than to erect deductive systems. They realized that science does not result in absolute truth, but is a human methodical approach to divine "revelation" in nature.'[3]

That the rationalistic approach properly used in conjunction with experimentation could lead to significant scientific advances was shown by Galileo. It doubtless gave rise to his mathematical approach and, combined with an emphasis on experimentation, was to lead to important discoveries. How theory combined with experiment are the essential ingredients for the development of science was exhibited in Galileo's careful investigations. Other features of Galileo's thought were not so commendable, for with Galileo also began the development of a view whereby God became merely the original Creator of the interacting atoms. Nature once created was considered to be independent and self-sufficient. This trend became more marked in the seventeenth century when the mediaeval and Reformation emphasis on God's direct and active relationship with His world began to be ignored. It is not surprising then that we soon find the Cartesian dualism emphasizing that the sequence of events in the world is determined by mechanical law and not divine action.

If the mathematical approach to nature is displayed by Galileo and Kepler, the empiricist experimental tradition finds its champions in men like Francis Bacon. To Baconians nature was not 'logical' and 'rational', but 'given'. According to Bacon we forfeit our dominion over nature by wanting to make her conform to our rationalistic prejudices, instead of adapting our conceptions to the data of observation and experiment. Hooykaas has made this aspect of Bacon's thought stand out in greater relief by contrasting it with the view of Simon Grynaeus of Basel (1550), a friend of Calvin. As Hooykaas puts it,

> 'Grynaeus, as well as Bacon, regarded the discovery of new parts of the earth as evidence of the restoration of our dominion over nature, but Bacon stresses the submission to facts, however *unexpected* they may be, whereas Grynaeus passes by this humiliating situation and glories in the fact

[3] *Ibid.*, p. 17.

that the human mind, by means of mathematics and astronomy, had in a certain respect anticipated these discoveries and travelled through the universe without needing immediate observation. He merely exults in the strength of human reason and laments, not that we overestimated this faculty, but that we left it unused.

'Bacon learned the lesson that we should "seek for the sciences not arrogantly in the little cells of human wit, but with reverence in the greater world". He expects the restoration of science to come by the liberation of the mind "from the serpent's venom that made it swell", and by "true humiliation of the spirit". Grynaeus, on the contrary, only finds opportunity to boast of the acuteness of human wit "which transcends the forces of nature".'[4]

As we move on into the seventeenth century we find Puritan scientists regarding science as an ally of true religion. In a spirit of optimism we find amongst the Puritans of all shades great protagonists of a free science. Very conscious of the dangers of appealing to any authority other than that of revelation they put their free science, 'not adorned by great names, but naked and simple',[5] over against the superstitious cult of Aristotle.

With the Enlightenment we find Newton, its great prophet, adhering to Baconian empiricist ideals in the face of the forces of rationalism and deism. Thus in 1713 he combats Cartesian necessitarianism on the same grounds on which Tempier in 1277 had condemned that of the Greeks and even of Aquinas. The same was to some extent true of the majority of eighteenth-century philosophers and scientists, accepting as they did the necessity for empiricism, yet at the same time being in danger of submitting its fruits to the rationalistic spirit of the age and thus forfeiting something of the true freedom of science by undue submission to human reason. Hooykaas concludes that the Enlightenment may be considered a secularized puritanism; that the essential difference between the eighteenth-century Enlightenment and the Puritan Enlightenment was that to the Puritans it was not freedom which led to truth, but truth which led to freedom. Perhaps these different emphases reflect more basic convic-

[4] *Ibid.,* p. 19.
[5] N. Carpenter, *Philosophia Libera* (Oxoniae, 1622), *praef.,* quoted by Hooykaas, *op. cit.*

tions. In an age of optimism, as the eighteenth century was, it was no doubt natural to develop this excessive faith in reason, unless one's views on these larger issues were constantly brought to the bar of revelation. The Puritan view of man and his fallen state for their part constrained them to develop a much more realistic assessment of the place of unaided reason, that is reason unaided either by revelation in matters of faith or by observation and experiment in matters of science.

Later in the eighteenth century it was left to the Romantic poets to reassert God's immanence in His world. For them nature was no mere material for scientific analysis, but they found in it another aspect, its beauty, which spoke of a deeper spiritual reality. In the face of Laplace's perhaps exaggerated emphasis on the over-against-Godness of nature, leading as it did to a deterministic and reductionist view of nature as a self-sufficient machine, it is not surprising to see the Romantics reacting with a view verging on pantheism.

This spirit of optimism showed itself also in a desire to extend the methods of science to all problems and all realms of knowledge. Typical of this is Hume's view that an idea which cannot be traced to specific sense data is for him without significance— a true forerunner of the positivism of the 1920s. This view did not, of course, go unchallenged, for we find Kant asserting strongly the crucial part played by the mind of man in *supplying* the categories for grouping and interpreting the empirical data of science, rather than waiting for them to be supplied in some unspecified manner by the data itself.

Moving into the nineteenth century, yet another fairly widely accepted product of Aristotelian doctrine comes under scrutiny, and soon under fire. It seemed natural, *reasonable* to conclude from Aristotle's teaching that, since all living things are in some sense embodiments of eternal forms or unchanging essences, species are therefore also fixed and unchanging. Now, however, with Darwin's teaching, Aristotelian biology is shaken at its very foundations. What if species are not fixed? What if there is a measure of change from generation to generation? What Newton had done to Aristotelian physics, Darwin was about to do to Aristotelian biology. With this challenge Darwin, like Newton, was to produce work which became the point of departure for a new world-view. Newton's intelligently designed machine would under Darwin's influence acquire the properties of a dynamic and progressive process.

At the same time, perhaps strangely it may seem to us now, we find aspects of Darwin's views of man recapturing a Hebrew-Christian emphasis on the nature of man. Nature, said Darwin, *includes* both man and his culture. By contrast the Greek tendency, as we saw earlier, was to separate man from the rest of creation and to give him and his mind an arrogant, aristocratic place, over against nature. Darwinian views also challenged again any simple analogy of God as the 'Maker' of the universe, that is as an absentee landlord who had made the world and then left it to run autonomously.

For our present purposes, however, we note particularly how Darwin's views raised in an acute form the issue of what sort of conclusion can properly be drawn from the methods of science. Can the idea of progress, for example, as championed by so many in the nineteenth century, be derived from science? Can ethical norms be derived from a scientific theory? T. H. Huxley, for example, answered 'No'; Darwin and Spencer thought 'Yes'. Sides were certainly taken on this latter issue, both then and since. Another issue, which we shall take up in detail later when we discuss the 'God of the gaps', was sharpened up at this time. For as Darwin and those who followed him provided possible scientific explanations for features of the natural world hitherto not understood scientifically, so the places remaining, where, according to some apologists, God was still considered to act, were slowly eliminated. And all this had the wholesome effect of forcing, with a fresh urgency, consideration of the relation of God to His creation. Furthermore, since the scientific evidence for evolution was claimed variously to support naturalism, evolutionism and theism, this raised with a fresh urgency questions concerning the nature of the scientific enterprise and of the knowledge to which it gives rise. Could one, for example, legitimately extrapolate the theory into a metaphysic or not? Clearly some thought 'Yes', some 'No'. It is to these two recurring questions, of how we should understand the relationship of God to His creation, and how we should understand the scientific enterprise and the knowledge to which it gives rise, that we shall turn in the next two chapters.

CHAPTER 2

GOD, CREATION AND THE LAWS OF NATURE

IN order to make sense of the range and variety of experience which we gain every day of our lives, we all find it necessary to make use of some form or other of organizing and storing such experience. We may regard these shorthand accounts as thought-models, and most of us make use of them most of the time. Some become highly organized, systematized and quite explicit; others remain vague and often implicit. The aim and function of them all is to produce a consistent and non-contradictory structure, which co-ordinates and makes sense of all our knowledge and experience. They vary enormously, of course, in their degree of complexity. Often children and primitive peoples will use very simple and concrete pictures. At the other end of the continuum we find mathematical physicists employing highly abstract and complex models.

What is true of our experience in general is also true of our experience and knowledge of the natural order in particular, and if we stop to think about it at all, we shall see that it is true also of our thinking about God and His relation to His creation. As we saw in the last chapter, a wide range of different thought-models has been proposed and defended down the centuries concerning the relation of God to His creation. In a sense the emergence of each new model served to underline the fact that any model, however refined, is never fully adequate for the task. And arising out of these models a range of different views concerning the meaning and the status of the so-called laws of nature has been propounded.

We shall select only two of the many models that have been used in the past, and we shall select them partly by way of illustration, and partly because these two models in differing guises have recurred from time to time and, when taken to extremes, have been responsible for producing unbalanced views of the relation of God to His creation.

We saw in the previous chapter how the picture of God as the 'divine mechanic' or 'machine-tender' emerged and changed in different periods. The main properties of this sort of model, which we shall call the craftsman model, are derived from our human experience of what it means to create something out of existing materials, whether it be an instrument or a complicated machine. According to this thought-model, God the Creator is conceived as an infinitely wise and clever inventor and constructor, who has, at some point in time, produced the universe as we know it and has set it running. It is usually also implied that once the machine 〜 *been* set running, it is to all intents and purposes autonomous, 〜 occasional *interventions* when some particular 〜 about or some servicing of the machine

DEVINE

ACTIVITY

〜 applied in the theological context we find 〜 ndue emphasis on two aspects of God's 〜 n. In the first place, it may tend to over- 〜 fness from that which He has created, and 〜 plies that it is necessary for God to intervene from 〜 order to bring about occasional unexpected occurrences for His particular purposes, and that it is only on these occasions that we may properly see His divine activity. The most celebrated and widely known of the models of this kind was the one proposed by Paley, who regarded God as the watchmaker, and that which He created as the watch. Such a view leads to a false kind of supernaturalism, in that it suggests that God's activity in the created world should be looked for and discerned mainly in occasional acts from without, which are injected into the otherwise autonomous orderly working of the machine. In short, models of this kind encourage a philosophy of nature which regards it simply as an autonomous machine which needs no divine sustaining activity to keep it in existence from moment to moment. So for God to bring about events which are commonly considered to be miraculous, He must return and intervene in a system which He has previously set going and then left.

Another feature of models of this kind is that the craftsman, or the mechanic who makes artefacts, makes them primarily for their use as a means to an end. They are not an end in themselves. As a result such creations can hardly be said to express in themselves very much of the personality of the craftsman or the mechanic. Such models therefore encourage one to ignore or at least minimize questions concerning the purpose for which the created order exists.

There are, however, certain aspects of this model which do focus our attention on important theological truths. Thus it reminds us that the purpose of any instrument or machine lies outside the actual constitution and mechanism of the machine itself; the purpose in fact lies solely in the mind of the creator and not within that which is created. In short, this may teach us that the creation remains instrumental to God's ultimate purposes, and that it is designed to achieve an end beyond itself. The Westminster Confession puts it succinctly when it reminds us that God created the world 'for the manifestation of the glory of His eternal power, wisdom and goodness'.

The second group of models which have occurred from time to time serves to call to mind the picture of God as a creative artist, and as such conjures up for us a different set of ideas. Models of this kind found an early champion in Dorothy Sayers[6] and in recent years have been developed by writers such as MacKay. Certain features of such a model immediately contrast with ones that we noted concerning the craftsman model. For example, in general, a work of art finds its value within itself, rather than in any instrumental use to which it is put. As a work of art it exists for enjoyment and admiration more than for use. Moreover, the inherent value of a work of art is usually considered to lie, first in what it reveals of the truth which the artist feels he needs to express, and second in what it may express of the character of the artist himself. Immediately we must note that God does not, as does the artist, *need* to create in order to understand more clearly for Himself the truth which He wishes to express. God creates from pure love of creation. Even so there is

[6] Dorothy Sayers, *Unpopular Opinions* (Gollancz, 1946).

scriptural warrant for saying that in a sense God also may con-
template His works and say, as is said in Genesis, that it is 'very
good' (Gn. 1:31). We also note that the distinction drawn a
moment ago between revealing some aspect of the truth and
expressing the character of the artist disappears when we think
of God's creative activity. In His creation God certainly reveals
something of His majesty and power and Godhead, as we are
taught in Romans 1, but this revelation is also an expression of
His character. Models of this kind clearly lay much greater
emphasis upon the immanence of God than the craftsman type of
model which emphasizes His transcendence. Along with this
emphasis on God's immanence comes the danger that, when it is
extended beyond its primary purpose, it can all too easily slip
into one of many different varieties of pantheism.

In order to do full justice to our understanding of the relation
of God to His creation, we may need to use a wide variety of
models, each of which attempts to make clearer one aspect of
this relationship. We may note that both of these groups of
analogies or models, the craftsman type and the creative artist
type, without further development share one radical shortcoming
in that they fail to do justice to the clear biblical teaching that
God continues to sustain the universe and to hold it in being
moment by moment. The two groups of models we have mentioned so far both leave us with a picture of the creator, whether
he be a craftsman or an artist, completing his instrument or his
work of art and then leaving it at that. How may we come a little
nearer to doing justice to the continuing activity of God in relation
to His creation? It was at this point that the conference found
MacKay's detailed elaboration of Dorothy Sayers's approach
both helpful and in some of its aspects controversial.

According to one variant of this model we may adapt our
thinking about creative artistry to make use of modern techno-
logical developments of the mid-twentieth century. Imagine that
instead of our artist using canvas and oils, he uses a television
screen to display his creation and he uses the transmitting apparatus of the television station in order to generate the display
which he wishes to portray to us upon his screen. The important
difference between this variant of the creative artist model and
the one we described earlier is that the picture on the screen

continues to exist and continues to have its present form only so long as our creative artist is continuing to generate the programme which is the expression of his mind. The moment he stops generating his programme our picture ceases to exist. Certainly this model helps to rectify the misrepresentation of our earlier creative artist model, in that it underscores the continuing activity of the artist in holding his creation in being from moment to moment.

Even so, this model of the creative artist still had one major inadequacy, which MacKay tackled in order to approximate a little more closely to the true biblical picture of God's relation to His creation.

We must first of all recall how the Bible opens with a narrative about the creative activity which gives rise to the existence of our world and of ourselves. The Bible reminds us frequently (*e.g.* Col. 1:17; Heb. 1:3) that not only do the objects of creation, including ourselves, owe their continuing existence to the activity of the creative Word, but also the whole space-time meshwork of events are 'upheld' and 'cohere' by and in the same creative Word. More important still, the biblical picture teaches us that our Creator is active within the drama of our existence not only in His creative sustaining power moment by moment, but also in some mysterious way in His personal Self-revelation. In MacKay's words:

> 'Our Creator is more than simply the Creator of our drama, he is also the Creator-participant. With this in mind we must also note that nothing that we say on the one hand about our createdness, must be allowed to distort or diminish the truth which is conveyed to us on the other hand, in the many complementary pictures, which depict us as children of a loving father, as sheep that have gone astray, as prodigal sons offered a loving welcome in the home of our father.'

Let us see now how MacKay complicated his earlier analogy of the creative artist in order to come a little nearer to the biblical picture of God not only as Creator, but also as Creator-participant in His creation. 'Let us imagine', he wrote, 'the relationship of the author, as a creator, to the literary work which he creates. We can notice certain relevant features of this at once, such as that our author when he eventually conceives and utters his literary work, does so as a single coherent picture including the past, present and future of the characters of his story, and the world in which he sets them.' And, as we shall discover, this fact alone may help us to appreciate the logical distinction between the standpoint of the creator of the drama, who is in this sense a spectator, and that of the actor within the drama. We shall later pursue in some detail this matter of the logical relations between creator-talk and creature-talk, but for the moment we simply wish to note that it is a distinction which must be made.

In seeking to adapt this picture to do justice to the biblical teaching, MacKay asked us to imagine a character in our literary work who finds himself addressed by his fellow-characters, some of whom claim to speak to him in the name of his creator and their creator. This refers, of course, to the way in which from time to time the prophets spoke and prefixed their statements with words such as 'thus says the Lord . . . '. 'Most amazing of all', wrote MacKay, 'the character in our literary work suddenly finds himself confronted by, and personally addressed by, a fellow character who claims to be identical with the creator of the whole literary work and all its characters. Here we are already involved in the mystery of the Incarnation.' In this way MacKay steadily adapted and complicated the picture of the creative literary artist, in order to do justice to the biblical teaching which declares that God in eternity, our Creator, is also identical with the One 'who spoke by the prophets', who was in Christ reconciling the world to Himself, and who still today continues to invite personal dialogue and personal relationships with the creatures whom He has made.

Since from time to time in later sections of this book we shall have occasion to refer back to this creator-participant model of MacKay's, let us now briefly draw attention to certain important features of it, which may help us in disentangling, or at least setting into a new perspective, some of the recurring debates concerning topics like free will and determinism, providence, and the laws of nature. Let us note that this picture should alert us to distinguish carefully at all times the different logical standpoints of the creator and his creatures, and this is especially important whenever we are tempted to oppose improperly creator-talk and creature-talk.

We noted a few moments ago that from the creator's viewpoint his work is created as a space-time unity; it is created as a whole, he creates the space-time framework of his production, and not only does he create the scenery, the setting, and the characters of his work, but also and more significantly he creates the events that occur. It is not that he creates the characters, the scenery and the environment of his work and then leaves them to interact according to some 'natural law' apart from his control, but much more significantly he creates the events past, present and future, and holds the whole thing in being from moment to moment in this sense. At the same time, while he does indeed create the time-scale in which the events of his characters take place, he also undertakes his own creative activity *outside* of this creaturely time scale. Since our main concern in this particular chapter is how the Christian model of the relation of God to His creation encourages us to conceptualize the so-called laws of nature, and the implications of this for questions of miracles, we shall not explore the details of this model further now, but shall see how it is relevant to these particular problems.

THE LAWS OF NATURE

It is often asserted that you cannot believe in the lawfulness of the natural order and also in miracles, and in discussions concerning these topics there are a number of questions which always seem to be raised, although the form may vary from time to time. The sorts of question we have in mind are those which ask whether belief in the lawfulness of nature *leaves room* for God to *intervene* in the natural order. Or again, there are those who raise the question of whether (or even assert that) God *uses* natural laws in order to bring about His creative purposes. Or again there are those who ask whether we should regard miracles as God *intervening* from time to time in the otherwise orderly working of creation. Many will recognize how these questions are solemnly asked and often firmly answered one way or the other. Yet if the sort of approach we have begun to outline above approximates to the truth, then, as MacKay has emphasized, the phrases such as *leaving room* for God, or God *using* natural laws, or God *intervening* must all stem from a model or models of God's relation to

His creation which are themselves inadequate. Indeed, they may not even be merely inadequate, but may on closer scrutiny lead to conclusions which are frankly misleading.

The point is that since according to the Bible nothing continues to exist, nothing continues in being, apart from God's moment-to-moment activity, it therefore becomes meaningless to ask whether the laws of nature *leave room* for God's activity. How could they *leave room* for God's activity, since God's activity is present all the time? Or again how could God *intervene* and *suspend* His laws from time to time, since He is there all the time holding everything in existence? In what sense could God *use* natural laws, since natural laws are only our way of summarizing our experience of the regular occurrence of events in the creation which God holds in being all the time? So it is that each of the expressions, *leaving room, intervening* and *using,* may be seen to be condoning a radical misconception of the relation of God the Creator to the created order. As creatures we must take what is given, and in seeking to understand what is given we may indeed summarize our experience partly in terms of what we call natural laws. Such a view as this, which we believe to be the biblical view, means that since the whole pattern of space-time events is not only conceived but also held in being moment by moment by God, we should therefore not regard what we term miraculous events as interventions. They are in fact no more and no less dependent upon God's activity than day-to-day occurrences which we take so readily for granted.

Let us try to make a little clearer what we have in mind by referring back to and adapting slightly the model of the electronic artist introduced earlier in this chapter. Consider the situation in which we may be watching a television production of a new play. Let us also suppose that the play is written and produced by the owner-operator of the television transmitting network. As we watch this production we are shown a long sequence of a hitherto unknown game—cricket—and, being intrigued by this game and being interested in playing it ourselves, we watch it very carefully and make detailed notes of the things which happen and eventually we believe that we have deduced the rules of the game from observing carefully the regularities in the events which have occurred in the game. Our position as viewers of this performance is in some important respects similar to our activity as scientists, who observe the events in God's creation and then attempt to discover the rules of how these events hang together. Of course, in other respects this picture is inadequate since, in general, as scientists we not only observe, but we also manipulate the events, and this we cannot do in our analogy.

In a very limited sense the owner-operator-author and producer of the production that we have been observing on our television screen has similarities with God's creative sustaining activity of the events in the world around us, since if the transmitting station were to stop, there would be nothing left for us to go on observing. The show would be over. Regarded in this way our discovery of the regularities in the events we have been observing means that for us natural laws are *descriptive* rather than *prescriptive,* and emerge for us only *post hoc,* as features of and within the created order. With this particular picture in mind let us now reconsider the question of miracles.

MIRACLES RECONSIDERED

According to the view outlined above it should be clear that it is not only improper, but also mistaken, to focus attention on miracles entirely or even principally on the grounds that they give *factual* evidence for divine activity. If we give full weight to the biblical assertions about God's divine upholding of all things at all times, then both the events that we label miraculous, as well as the non-miraculous events, are equally dependent for their occurrence upon the same creative power of God. If then we are not to focus our attention solely or even principally upon the lack of correspondence to known scientific laws of events that we label miraculous, what aspect of these events should we focus our attention upon? A short answer to this question would be upon the mode or purpose of God's activity in those events that we consider to be miraculous. Before discussing miraculous events further, we had perhaps better try to clarify our use of the term 'miracle', following the position taken by Pinnock in his conference paper.

Since all events are dependent upon God's continuing activity, it seems best to reserve the term 'miracle' for those events which reverse the normal observations or expectations of man. We can then retain the term 'providence' to cover the daily gifts which we are constantly receiving at God's hands. We should perhaps at this point attempt to summarize how the occurrence and function of miracles are portrayed to us in the biblical record. The first thing that we notice is that the Bible does not focus our attention upon the relation of an event which we call a miracle to the natural order, but rather upon the impression which that event has made upon the minds of those who witnessed it (e.g. Mk. 3:11; Ex. 14:31). We find also that the relation which the miraculous events bear to the wider purposes of God's revelation of His will to men is emphasized, when such events occur in the biblical narrative. The biblical use of miracles therefore serves to focus our attention, not upon theoretical questions as to whether the cause of a miracle is regular but still unknown to us, or whether it is in some way contrary to our normal expectations, but rather upon the direct impression that the event makes upon those who witness it.

An examination of the Bible soon convinces us that to label an event as miraculous does not imply that there are no known natural causes for that event. On some occasions we are in fact invited to notice the natural cause which was responsible for the event. Thus the crossing of the Red Sea is especially instructive in this regard, since the cause of the rolling back of the waters is stated in Exodus 14:21 to be a strong east wind. This aspect of the occurrence of miracles has encouraged some people to regard some miracles as divine coincidences. It does, however, remain the case that it is only against the backdrop of what we have already come to expect of the regular workings of creation that we can perceive the unusual events to which we attach particular significance and may regard as miracles.

Miracles are certainly not invasions by God into the otherwise natural working of creation, for this would deny that in some sense God is there already. Neither are they merely natural, if by this it is meant to imply that God is not active in the whole stream of events moment by moment. They are rather special acts of God and seen to be such, but ones in which the secondary means which are responsible for the event are neither more nor less given by Him than any other day-to-day occurrence.

It may perhaps be helpful to notice that there are some miracles which are characterized primarily by some unusual awe-inspiring and distinctive feature, which may result in their being regarded as omens or portents of something yet to occur (*e.g.* Elijah on Mount Carmel). Miracles of this type, as Pinnock pointed out, certainly serve to exercise a magnetic attraction upon men's attention, but their primary purpose is to fix men's attention upon the message that accompanies the event. Events of this kind are open for the eyes of all to see, and are not events which are seen as miraculous only through the eyes of faith. It is clear from the Old Testament record that the history of Israel, with its miraculous preservation over the centuries, certainly excited the admiration of the people of surrounding unbelieving nations, as is made clear in Joshua 2 : 10. A second recurring feature of some miracles is the way in which they are seen as mighty acts of divine power. Thus, to quote from Pinnock's paper,

> 'The mighty acts of Jesus were performed by One who is Himself called the power of God, and these works were entirely appropriate actions to be performed by One who was both Man and God. As some have put it, they served for him as credentials in the midst of an unbelieving generation.'

Finally, another pervading characteristic of miracles is their importance as signs, or tokens, or pledges of an age yet to come. Indeed some would focus upon this aspect of miracles as the most important aspect, that in every case they point forward to what is yet to come in the purposes of God, and this is true both in the Old and in the New Testaments. Regarded in this way the healing miracles may be considered as the temporary rolling back of the claims of death, which will one day be abolished.

It may be instructive to summarize what we have said by drawing attention to the miracle of healing recorded in the third chapter of the Acts of the Apostles, where we can observe all three of these features of miracles that we have mentioned. Thus we are told that those who observed the miracle were filled with wonder and amazement, and we also find that the apostles make it clear that this mighty act of divine power was, as they put it, 'not by our own power', but by the power of Christ; and finally we may see this as a healing miracle, as a sign and a pledge of an age yet to come, when all disease and sickness will be done away with.

It is sometimes not realized how relatively scarce the miracles are within the biblical narrative as a whole. To put it another way, if we were today writing a narrative with the express intention of impressing our readers with the other-worldliness of the events that were portrayed, and the claims that were made for what was said, we should be sorely tempted to see that our narrative was well stocked throughout with miraculous events, which would not allow our readers ever to forget the divine origin of that which we were trying to convey. By contrast, when we consider the thousands of years covered by the biblical narrative, we find that this is not the case, but that the miraculous events are surprisingly scarce. Thus we find that they tend to concentrate around three major eras in the total biblical record, namely around the events of the Exodus of the people of Israel from Egypt, around the time of the proclamation of the prophets of the ninth century BC, and lastly around the apostolic era recorded in the New Testament. But it is worthy of note that such outstanding characters in the biblical record as Jeremiah and David, for example, do not have events of a miraculous kind attributed to them.

It should also be pointed out that it is difficult to provide a strong case from the biblical records to suggest that miracles should be used in any sense as knock-down arguments or incontrovertible proofs. This is not to forget that on one occasion they are described as 'many infallible proofs' (Acts 1:3, AV). It is almost certainly the case, however, that we are too readily reading into the word *proof* a meaning which is familiar to us today in a juridical sense or even in a scientific sense, but which was probably quite foreign to the minds of the first- and second-century writers. If this is so, then the function of miracles should be regarded not as providing incontrovertible proofs, but as events which bear witness to the divine character of something that is being proclaimed, and/or of the person who is proclaiming the message. Another aspect of this same point is that whatever factual event occurs there may still be many differences of interpretation. As Aristotle put it many years ago, 'It is not the facts which divide men but the interpretation of the facts.' To make this point abundantly clear we could realistically assert that had a confirmed atheist been present at a resurrection appearance of Christ, he might, on the basis of his own presuppositions, quite reasonably have exclaimed simply, 'I always thought there might be such things as ghosts but now I am convinced.' The point is that he would not of necessity have been constrained to interpret such a resurrection appearance as evidence for the divinity of Christ, but rather that ghosts exist. This, of course, serves to draw attention to the fact that many people do turn away from the idea of miracles, not because they are scientists, but because their world-view begins by being atheistic. In fact it is true to say that on close examination the Christian view of miracles is found to be more open-minded than the non-theistic point of view. The point, of course, is that while observation can tell us what has happened, it cannot tell us what could have happened.

Since it is so often asserted and too easily accepted that to start from a non-theistic point of view is more open-minded than to start from a Christian point of view, perhaps we should expand a little on some features of one particular non-theistic point of view by way of illustration of this particular point.

Such a point of view was developed in an extreme form in the philosophy of Hume, and summarized at the conference by Leith. It would not be appropriate for us to digress at this point to consider in detail Hume's views, but we simply draw attention to the fact that it is not sufficiently well appreciated that to start from a non-theistic point of view, as he did, is not to start *without* presuppositions, but rather to start with *a different set* of presuppositions. Moreover such presuppositions are not themselves deducible from science, as is sometimes pretended. On a close examination of the two salient premises of the non-theistic world-view proposed by Hume, we find that the question of miracles could not even be discussed as a live issue since they were excluded by definition. What we mean is this. In the first place, Hume asserted that any report of a miraculous event is to be deemed less credible than a description of it as a rare (but in fact regular) natural event. His reason is that witnesses reporting the event are less reliable than the appearance of regularity in nature, which is all around us and which we have already accepted as infallible.

This leads on to the second premise, which is the idea that the uniformity of nature shall therefore be defined and accepted in such a way as to exclude the possibility of miracles. In contrast to this the Christian viewpoint we maintain is more open-minded, in that in the first place it agrees that it is perfectly legitimate to assume uniformity in nature, but at the same time it is willing to entertain the possibility of miracle, if there are found to be good historical grounds for doing so. In other words, our conception of natural laws accepts the fact that they are based on a comparatively small number of observations or experiments, and that they must always remain subservient to, rather than normative over, any further observations. Accordingly the theist is found to be more open-minded towards the historical material than the non-theist who must, because of his presuppositions, do his utmost to explain away the historicity of the record of any events which do not fit with his presuppositions. Moreover he will do this because he is already committed to a metaphysical principle of uniformity.

In conclusion, it may be helpful to set out briefly some implications which the view of miracles presented in this chapter carries for the way in which miracles may be presented in the proclamation of the Christian message and in apologetics. The progression from unbelief to belief may be regarded, from the human standpoint, as involving in the first place an acquaintance with a minimum of information about the Christian gospel, so that in the light of this minimum of information it seems reasonable and fair-minded at least to consider the possibility that the message of the gospel may be true. Following upon this it is frequently the case that the testimony of others who have walked this way before, and who have become Christians, and who now believe in miracles, will help the inquirer at least to consider the reasonableness of the theistic point of view. By implication this carries with it the realization that if the Christian view of God and His relation to His creation is at all correct, then God not only can, but may, do miracles from time to time, and that these unusual events may appear to be contrary to our normal day-to-day experience. When a person becomes a Christian and reads and studies the biblical record in the new light given to him through his relationship with Christ, then he begins to see the events which are called miracles from a different point of view. In presenting the Christian message there seems very little constraint from within the biblical record itself to adopt the reverse order to the one just outlined, for that would be to insist that a person must believe that this, that, or the other miracle occurred before he can begin to become a Christian. In fact such an approach would by experience seem to be patently self-defeating.

CHAPTER 3

THE SCIENTIFIC ENTERPRISE

THE APPROACH OF THE SCIENTIST

THE world we live in confronts us on every side with the achievements of the scientists. The motor cars we drive, the radios we listen to, the televisions that we watch, the jet aeroplanes flying overhead, the medical discoveries which alleviate our sickness, the new methods in education which make learning more rapid : all of these, and many other aspects of modern life, are a direct result of the activities of scientists in various disciplines. Since modern man owes so much to the scientists for his creature comforts, for his health and his enjoyment, it is not in the least surprising that his view of science is as high as it is. By comparison with the solid achievements of science, the achievements and the benefits of the arts, the humanities and religion must inevitably seem meagre and ephemeral. It should occasion no surprise therefore to discover that science has become, in the popular mind, as one writer has put it, a sacred cow. A cow, moreover, which if fed appropriately and milked in the proper way will continue to yield beneficial results for the good of all mankind. Add to all this the fact that in the teaching of science we must, almost of necessity, limit our laboratory exercises to straightforward and relatively simple experiments which give easily gathered, clear-cut results, and it becomes almost inevitable that science should be regarded as the mechanical application of a foolproof method, which by its nature will generate secure, unchanging results.

Such a view, as we shall see later, is reinforced by the manner in which the results of the activities of research scientists must be reported in the various scientific journals. In such reporting, in the interests of efficiency of communication and limitations of space, we aim at removing the personal element completely, and we set out our methods, results and conclusions in as concise and unambiguous a way as possible. All the ineffective methods we tried and discarded, all the blind alleys we went up in our efforts to interpret our results, and all the intuition, imagination and casual discussions with colleagues at conferences which affected every part of our work, must be studiously omitted from our reporting, and properly so in the interests of clarity and conciseness. And yet any scientist who is actively engaged in research knows full well that to build one's conception of the nature of science and of the methods which it employs solely on the basis of the reports published in scientific journals produces a complete misrepresentation of what really happens in the progress of science.

Is there such a thing as 'the scientific method'?

Neither is such an over-formalized view of the nature of science and of the scientific method confined to the popular press or to the popular imagination. It is increasingly the view being presented in some courses in the philosophy of science, in discussions of the scientific method and in some scientific textbooks. Once again the reasons for this are not difficult to find. The most obvious one is that the philosopher of science and the person who is trying to understand the logic of the scientific method inevitably look at the *post hoc* idealized model of what the scientist has been doing as he finds it portrayed in scientific papers.

Descriptions of this kind usually talk about *the* scientific method and portray it as the collection of data by means of observation and experiment, on the basis of which tentative hypotheses are formulated; these hypotheses are then tested further and their implications for new experiments can thus be seen. This process continues and gradually an hypothesis is substantiated or invalidated by further study. As the hypothesis becomes modified and extended to a widening range of observations it will eventually be given the name of a theory, and even ultimately a law. In practice, however, the two main components of this method, namely the experimental side of science and the theoretical side, are by

no means so easily separated, nor can the logical steps between
the two be so easily distinguished.

The popular view of science also portrays it as being based
always and solely upon precise observation, so that the scientist
is supposed to deal with 'pure facts', which will then yield indubit-
able, objective and impersonal knowledge. But of course there
are no such things as uninterpreted facts. It is not necessary to be
a psychologist to know that all of our experience is organized on
the basis of our particular interests, and that we selectively attend
to certain features of our environment and ignore the rest. This,
of course, applies in science also. We decide to pay attention to
certain variables, and as far as possible select these from other
variables which we choose to ignore. But already we have brought
in our judgments based on our earlier experience which has led us
to decide which data we shall pay attention to and which we shall
ignore.

The over-formalized statement of the scientific method thus
becomes characterized as the routine application of a set formula,
namely the systematic re-enactment of observation, formation of
hypotheses, testing of hypotheses, exploring the implications of
the hypotheses in experiments, retesting, and so on. Those who so
characterize the scientific method also often put forward an
extreme objectivist view of the knowledge which is derived by the
application of this method. Some who take such an extreme
objectivist view also regard the only statements which have any
meaning as being those which can be empirically verified, and go
on to insist that there is no possibility of valid knowledge other
than scientific knowledge. They also assert that, by sharing such
verification among a large number of persons, greater objectivity
is thereby achieved and that, in the course of such sharing, the
knowledge thus accumulated has gained an impersonal character
about it. On this view, there is a contrast between the scientific
procedure and the knowledge that is gained by its use, and the
erroneous hit-or-miss quality of personal judgments, and it is
only the former which will, so it is said, provide objective, factual
and reliable knowledge.

Clearly we would not wish to debate the *relative* objectivity,
the *relatively* impersonal quality of scientific knowledge. We
would, however, wish to debate some of the assumptions that are

made in this approach, such as that the only meaningful statements that we can make are scientific statements; that scientific statements are fundamentally non-subjective, completely impersonal; that there is an infallible procedure which is called *the* scientific method, which properly applied leads in regular fashion to discovery of truth; that no valid knowledge is obtainable without the use of this method. And arising out of all these, the implication that things like our subjective experiences, personal choices, our states of mind, and other things which at the moment cannot be subjected to the scientific method, can therefore have no valid meaning. Proponents of such an objectivist position set themselves to establish that there is and can be no personal coefficient in scientific knowledge. Such a view is often held with such tenacity that it acquires both the form and the force of a set of religious beliefs. At the centre of this position is the failure to consider the participation of the knower in that which he knows. And it is this point which, as we shall show later, is systematically attacked by Polanyi[7] in his book *Personal Knowledge*.

Against this over-formalized view of science a more realistic view soon becomes apparent from even a cursory reading of the history of science. It is soon clear that there is no royal road in scientific research which leads automatically and inevitably from observation to theory. At every stage in the process we must *decide* which of the many aspects of reality which confront us we shall seek to isolate for our detailed study, and this means that right from the very beginning of our search our data are in a sense 'theory laden'. We never seek to collect *all* the facts, but rather we decide that a particular aspect of the physical world is of significance because of some interest we have developed. We then seek to collect, either by observation or by experiment, those facts which we believe will enable us to understand better the aspects of reality which we are studying.

The data that the scientist deals with are not even always publicly verifiable in the way it is sometimes suggested. They are publicly verifiable only by those who have the competence and the training, and often also the appropriate equipment, to verify the facts which are being studied. Early on in any scientific investigation it becomes necessary to create our own conceptual terms

[7] M. Polanyi, *Personal Knowledge* (Routledge, 1958).

and to state as clearly as possible what we mean by these and how we intend to use them, since these conceptual terms as such are not part of the reality we observe, they are not directly observable, they are not given to us by nature, but they are created by us for the purposes of our investigations. The next stage may be to seek to correlate the observations that we make in such a way that we can see the way in which several different concepts are related systematically and we may then describe this systematic relationship as a law. When we have studied the particular phenomena for long enough we may have discovered a whole set of interrelated laws about the phenomena and we may then seek to bring these into a unified and generalized whole, which may be referred to as a theory.

In the formation of such theories, however, there is a constant interaction between a variety of activities and processes. On the one hand, we may begin by gathering sets of data which we think will be relevant, and then we may look for uniformities within these data. By processes of induction we may be able to reduce these uniformities to certain general laws which summarize in an economical way the observations that we have made. It is certainly clear that the scientific approach, even at this level, does not consist merely of the collection and cataloguing of facts. This in itself could never produce a scientific theory. It is the mental constructs which we bring to bear upon these facts which could be the beginnings of a theory. In addition we must remember the importance of deductive thinking in the development of science. It is certainly true that, once we have formed a preliminary generalization, we may then, on the basis of this generalization, make certain deductions concerning what may follow if our theory is true. But it must always be remembered that we never start simply from hypotheses; it is data that we start from.

Although an account of scientific activity in terms of the use of induction and deduction, combined with observation and experiment, would go a long way to describing the activity of many scientists, it would still leave out those breakthroughs which occur from time to time and which, possibly because of our present ignorance, we label as creative and imaginative acts.

How such creative thinking begins and is sustained is itself a matter for scientific study. It looks very much as if one of the crucial factors is seeing the relevance to the field in which one is working of a discovery in some other field or fields, and that this relevance brings completely new light onto an otherwise familiar problem. One thing, however, is clear, that in the course of any scientific inquiry there is a wide range of different mental operations which cannot be reduced to a single ideal type without failing to do justice to the richness and complexity of what is really happening.

This perhaps is another way of saying that scientific investigation is a very human activity, with the personality, ideals, interests, aspirations and many other things coming in at every point along the line. Coulson, who has argued this very convincingly, has pointed out that the attitudes and the experience of the scientists researching at the frontiers of knowledge are in stark contrast with the over-formalized account of science mentioned above. He has pointed out that they, more than anyone, are aware of the many non-scientific factors which contribute heavily to the success or failure of their endeavours. He has written,

> 'Think for a moment of some of the attitudes of mind with which any scientist comes to his search : with honesty, and integrity, and hope : there is enthusiasm, for no one ever yet began an experiment without an element of passion : there is an identification of himself with the experiment, a partisan character about his secret hopes for its conclusion which not even an adverse result can wholly extinguish : there is a humility before a created order of things, which are to be received and studied : there is a singleness of mind about the search which reveals what the scientist himself may often hesitate to say, that he does what he does because it seems exciting and it somehow fulfils a deep part of his very being : there is co-operation with his fellows, both in the same laboratory, and across the seven seas : there is patience akin to that which kept Madame Curie at her self imposed task purifying 8 tons of pitchblende to extract the few odd millegrams of radium : above all there is judgement—judgement as to what constitutes worthwhile research : judgement as to what is fit and suitable for publication. No wonder that a modern scientist—and no Christian either—has to say that "Science cannot exist without judgements of value".'[8]

[8] C. A. Coulson, *Science and Christian Belief* (Fontana Books, 1967), pp. 72-73.

In short, not only does the practice of science differ radically from the formal logical analysis of '*the* scientific method', but also, contrary to what is often asserted, we find scientists coming to their tasks with many different presuppositions. Clearly there is no such thing as science without presuppositions.

Personal participation in the scientific enterprise

Not only is the popular view of science, and of the over-formalized statement of the scientific method which goes with it, misleading in that it misrepresents the practice of science, but accompanying it there is often found a view of the nature of scientific knowledge which is equally indefensible, but this time from a theoretical point of view. As we mentioned earlier, the leader of the attack on this level has been Polanyi in his book entitled *Personal Knowledge*. At the conference Polanyi's views were strongly championed by Thorson in the face, at times, of searching probing by some participants who felt that perhaps Polanyi ended up with a little too subjective an evaluation of scientific knowledge. Thorson pointed out that,

> 'As the title of his book suggests, Polanyi's major thesis is that there is no knowledge apart from knowers, and the personal participation of the knower in that which he knows is both pervasive and inescapable. This participation is not in itself explicit; indeed Polanyi shows that a major part of it is tacit, and cannot be explicit. Such a participation involves acts of commitment to those things which I, the knower, hold to be true. The objectivist notion of impersonal knowledge which requires no act of personal validation is analysed by Polanyi and destroyed in a systematic fashion. This analytical destructiveness, which is the first part of Polanyi's thinking, is relevant in that he takes the ideas of the well known objectivists and positivists, by which they purport to evade criteria of personal judgement in knowing, and he shows how in every case the inescapable personal involvement is hidden, either in descriptive terminology which turns out to be semantically dishonest, or more often in tacit assumptions which are communicated from one knower to another as the tacitly understood and accepted coefficients of what is being done explicitly.'

Polanyi begins his analysis by examining the claim of imper-sonal objective knowledge in the empirical sciences. His major thesis is that the personal participation of the knower in what he calls knowledge is both pervasive and completely inescapable. In developing this thesis Polanyi made three points which are of particular relevance to our discussion and were summarized by Thorson thus:

> 'He begins his analysis by examining the claim that there is impersonal objective knowledge derivable through the work of empirical scientists. This raises at once an issue which is the cornerstone of earlier forms of logical positivism, namely, what they call *the intersubjective verifiability criterion;* what we have referred to above as the objectivity that is achieved when verification is shared amongst a number of persons. Polanyi observes that the history of controversies in science, or even the everyday experience of teaching science and carrying out research, remind us that such a criterion depends upon prior training and an agreed competence amongst such observers. Thus the claim to intersubjective verifiability *really means* the kind of verification that is shared among a group of trained and skilled observers in particular disci-plines, who accredit their own and each other's competence, and whenever this interpersonal accreditation system breaks down controversy can immediately ensue. In the second place, he reminds us that in many sciences the results are presented in terms of conclusions which are given as possi-bilities, and it is a matter of personal judgement at what point one decides that the level of probability in a set of data is such that one is prepared to accept an implication said to be present in that data.'

(The continuing controversy over experiments in the field of extra-sensory perception illustrates this point extremely well.)

> 'The third important point is that smuggled into many of the major theoretical achievements that have been made in science is the claim that a particular theory has a rational beauty about it which satisfies the intellectual passions of the discoverer, and this beauty is accepted and accredited by him as far as he is concerned as the token of fittingness of external reality. Nowhere is this perhaps more marked than in the field of applied mathematics and mathematical phy-

sics, where it is not at all uncommon to find leaders in the field speaking freely of the *beauty, elegance* and *depth* of the methods which they develop. Polanyi, of course, readily accepts and realises that empirical observation is necessary in all scientific endeavour, but this is not the point under debate for him, rather it is to show the absurdity of the *extreme* positivist claim that things such as imagination and the appreciation of rational excellence and beauty play no necessary role in scientific discovery. To assert that scientific theories are somewhat like telephone directories, and no more than economical descriptions of facts obtained by the empirical testing of hypotheses selected at random, is such a distortion of the history of science, and of the experience of every research scientist, as to be nothing short of ridiculous. Yet this is precisely the claim of a rigorously impersonal logical positivism. Polanyi goes on to reinforce this point by reminding us of three periods in the rational conceptions of physics : the Pythagorean, based on geometry and numbers, the Newtonian based on the mechanics of systems of particles, and the modern based on systems of mathematical invariances. Each of these is more general and more sophisticated with respect to empirical observation than its predecessor, but each conveys criteria of rational beauty which for each period are standards to which the scientist is committed, as the token of reality. The description of theories by words which downgrade our recognition of this excellence, words like simple, symmetric and fruitful, is, he says, semantic dishonesty, and reflects the objectivist urge to deny personal participation in knowing truth. It is for these reasons and others that Polanyi finds an inescapable element of commitment in the search of the knower for knowledge.'

Does Polanyi go too far?

While Polanyi has thoroughly exposed and successfully criticized the extreme objectivist account of the scientific method and of the knowledge to which it gives rise, there are nevertheless certain features of his own view that should be scrutinized carefully. The most obvious one is the criticism that if we accept this position we must then face the question of how we can distinguish between that which we hold to be true and those beliefs which we regard as purely subjective or even deluded.

Polanyi would reply that the distinction between pure subjectivity on the one hand, and what a society may justly call knowledge on the other, depends entirely on the responsibility which he sees present in commitment to that which is considered to be real. The prime ingredients of this commitment as Polanyi sees it are, first, that I must distinguish between myself and that to which I am committed so that I recognize an external reality which retains its character in itself and independently of my subjective appreciation of it. Also I consider myself obliged to use my freedom to see properly what this reality is like, firmly believing that as long as I persist in my attempt to understand, I eventually shall do so. My commitment is properly to understand the reality that faces me, even though I am aware of the risk which is always present that I may see incorrectly. My responsibility, moreover, is not merely rational; it also involves my own relation to reality as I see it, and I must put into practice that which I do know and go on to attempt to verify the predictions of the insights gained so far. In addition, what I believe to be real because of my commitment I seek to share with others and to persuade them also of its pattern. In the final analysis I am always aware of the possibility that I may be wrong, but having consciously recognized this I may then go on in the conviction that the future will endorse my commitment by its outcome.

It could be argued still that to rely completely on the view of one's fellows would leave no room for creative thought and innovation and also that the sort of responsible commitment which is being spoken of, if it must be made by a group of individuals, could still be of such a kind which would never win a public opinion poll but nevertheless may be true. And finally it leaves wide open the possibility of wholesale cultural delusions. Polanyi realizes these difficulties and faces them squarely, and reiterates that it is just at this point that the element of risk involved must be squarely faced, in the conviction that with *continued* seeking these difficulties will be overcome.

THE NATURE OF SCIENTIFIC KNOWLEDGE

The last 100 years have seen some radical changes in the opinions held by scientists and philosophers concerning the nature of the knowledge to which the scientific enterprise gives rise. During the nineteenth century the truth, the certainty, and the exactness of physical knowledge had seemed to the majority to be beyond doubt or question. This may be seen in the frequent and over-ready use of terms such as 'objective' and 'the laws of nature' in the writings of that time, particularly as exemplified in those who shared the spirit of Laplace. At that time physical objects and phenomena were considered as existing and occurring within the framework of absolute time and space. It was assumed that the knowledge about these phenomena which could be acquired through the scientific procedure of observation, measurement and inductive reasoning might properly be called objective, in the sense that it was believed that it was completely determined by the object of the observations. This extreme objectivity in the observations and measurements that were made was carried over into the use made at that time of the term 'laws of nature'. The term became used in such a way that it seemed as if Nature herself was compelled to follow these laws in blind obedience. This objectivistic interpretation of physical knowledge found its major exponent in the idea of 'the spirit of Laplace' according to which, by knowledge of the positions and velocities of all material particles we should be able to predict the future as well as to reveal the past of the whole universe, the history of mankind included.

It is now well known, among scientists at least, that the advancement of physical science has itself provided reasons to criticize and revise this ultra-objectivist interpretation of physical knowledge. As Sizoo wrote in his conference paper,

> 'Under the pressure of the empirical facts, physicists them-selves recognized that the observing and the knowing *subject* could not be eliminated completely from the knowledge about the observed known *object*. . . . It is true, that in the theory of relativity, just as in classical physics, the observer is assumed to be able to observe and to measure without dis-turbing the state of the observed and measured object. How-ever, it is emphasized in this theory that experimental veri-fiability and measurability, are essential conditions in the definition of physical concepts and quantities.'

The developments in quantum physics have introduced the

observer in a still more fundamental way in the interpretation of physical knowledge so that, as Sizoo went on,

> 'This theory has indeed brought forward the insight that every physical observation must be considered as a discreet and unpredictable interaction between the observing subject and the observed object. The fact that in every physical measurement there must be an interaction between the measuring instrument and the system on which the measurement has to be performed was, of course, well known in classical physics. However, it was assumed that this interaction could in principle be reduced to zero and therefore be ignored in the theory. The discovery of Planck's constant, the quantum of action, led physicists to acknowledge that this reduction to zero did not correspond with physical reality and that they had to lay this lower limit of interaction at the basis of their theory.'

A second impact of the new look in physics was the discovery that at times in order to describe the full behaviour of both light and matter and their mutual interactions, the physical concepts of waves and particles had to be used alternately and in a complementary way. 'The result was', wrote Sizoo,

> 'that in modern physical thought the concept of continuity as well as that of discontinuity, the principle of causality as well as that of probability, are used on equal terms, representing a dual approach to physical phenomena which is needed to grasp their full reality. These two ways of approach, which in a merely logical sense may seem to be contradictory, are in fact correlated to two kinds of experiments, that is to two ways in which the observing subject may put himself in relation to the object to be observed, and which must supplement each other in the process of acquiring physical knowledge.'

Sizoo later observed that,

> 'These changes within the field of science itself did not fail to influence the ideas about the nature of physical knowledge. Whereas the objectivist conceptions had clearly to be abandoned, the subjectivist point of view became the new favourite. Perhaps the most extreme formulation of this conception was that given by Eddington in his proposition, that

"all the fundamental laws and constants of physics" can be deduced unambiguously from a priori considerations and therefore "are wholly subjective".'[9]

It still remains the case that there are strong subjective features in current views on the nature of physical science. It seems clear therefore that, as mentioned earlier when discussing Polanyi's views, personal involvement of the observer and of the knower is present even in the most objective of the physical sciences, but this should not lead us to embrace hastily an extreme subjectivist position as has been done by some religious people, because they see in it a solution for the difficulties they previously met in maintaining the reliability of religious knowledge. We should maintain that neither an extreme objectivist nor an extreme subjectivist position can be the basis for a Christian conception of the nature of physical knowledge. Such a basis can be found only in that knowledge about the world which comes to us other than through the methods of science. For 'the Bible does not bring forward the idea of God's creative activity as a philosophical concept, neither does it use the concept of "nature" as scientists do, to indicate the sum total of all observable phenomena' (Sizoo). The biblical assertion is that the things and phenomena which we can perceive around us have all been created and are being preserved by the one same Almighty God. And the biblical view would also hold that such order and uniformity which we observe and discover in the range and variety of the phenomena we examine are all determined by the same God. Man also being a part of creation is likewise dependent upon his Creator, but his position within the creation is unique in that in some sense he is unlike other creatures, being made after God's image and likeness, and as such has been given the special commission to have dominion over the rest of creation. This, of course, is not a statement that is made as the result of philosophical argument, but it is a statement given to us by God and one to which we can only assent in faith or reject. Nevertheless, for the Christian it does have significance for his philosophy of the nature of physical knowledge, for, as Sizoo pointed out,

'If we accept by faith the assertion that God created man

[9] A. Eddington, *The Philosophy of Physical Science* (CUP, 1938), p. 105.

after His image and likeness and placed him in this created world with the unique instruction to have dominion over it, this faith will engender within man the confidence that equipped with his sensory and intellectual faculties he may, by perceiving and studying the phenomena that surround him, prove to be so adjusted to these phenomena that he will be able to acquire the knowledge that he needs in order to carry out his cultural charge.'

Furthermore it seems clear that when this position is adopted,

'physical knowledge is found to have essentially the character of a qualified relation extending within the created order, between the intelligent subject, man, on the one hand, and the intelligible phenomena, the rest of nature, on the other' (Sizoo).

The ingredients in other kinds of knowing such as artistic, aesthetic, or religious, no doubt involve differing degrees of inter-action of the observer or the knower with that which he is observing or knowing. In his scientific activity man is engaged in actualizing this knowledge relation, potentially given by the Creator, and therefore, to quote again from Sizoo,

'whether he recognises this or not, he is engaged in fulfilling his cultural charge. According to this view the nature and content of the knowledge relation will be determined by the object as well as by the subject. The possibility of discovering and describing order, uniformity and constant relations within the phenomena, is certainly due to the nature of the object. But it must equally be due to the nature of the human intellect, which enables men to build up a scheme of logic-ally coherent concepts, which are adequately related to the features of the object. This conception means that the objectivistic as well as the subjectivistic interpretations of physical knowledge have both to be rejected in their extreme forms as being tendencies to ignore or anyhow to minimise the significance of one of the two poles between which the knowledge relation is established.'

In saying this we are not, of course, objecting to the common statement that, *relatively* speaking, physical science may be called pre-eminently objective, providing that, in this statement, the term objective does not mean independent of the subject, but points to the fact that physical knowledge can be formulated in such intelligible and logically coherent concepts that it can be transferred in a convincing way from one individual subject to another. And this, of course, is another way of saying what we have already said when discussing Polanyi's views, namely that one of the things which helps to increase objectivity is the intersubjective verifiability which is possible when acquiring knowledge of this kind.

Objectivity, commitment, personal and group values

One distinction must be made to avoid a possible misunderstanding in what we have said so far. Since science has a large *personal* element in it, it does not mean that it is *private*. Indeed one of its more important features is that there is an element of public sharing in that which is discovered, so that within the scientific community of those competent to judge, there is the constant provision for checking the assertions and the results claimed by one's fellow-scientists. The scientific community is international in scope and its members share a common tradition. This leads on to another aspect of science which increases our belief in its objectivity, and that is that those things which are discussed and reported have about them a certain universality. The scientist is committed to this universality, but even this involves him at the personal level, and again Polanyi's argument is relevant here since, to use his own phrase, 'there is the universal intent' of the commitment that the scientist makes that enables his personal involvement to contribute to the seeking of truth rather than the hindering of it. Such a commitment to objectivity, however, does not mean commitment to disinterestedness; indeed, the true scientist is passionately dedicated to the values he brings to his science and to the worthwhileness of his task.

As we move from the physical sciences to the biological sciences, and then on to the social and behavioural sciences, we find that the personal involvement of the knower seems to influence more and more the process of his inquiry. More and more he exercises his personal judgment in selecting, evaluating and interpreting his data. And it is in this way that we discover that the extent and the range of the involvement of the knower varies with the nature of the reality that he seeks to know. We can thus picture, as we mentioned earlier, a continuum with varying degrees of personal involvement. Such an idea of a continuum contrasts with the claim that we must make an absolute dichotomy between a purely impersonal and objective science on the one hand and a subjective sphere of personal selfhood on the other. To take up either side of this dichotomy and to ignore the other would be to take up either an existentialist position or a positivist position, and for reasons we have given earlier we find neither of these convincing.

In closing this chapter it may be helpful to examine a little more closely, with religious knowledge especially in mind, our suggestion that knowledge of all kinds may be regarded as an expression of a relationship between the knower and the known. We have suggested that we may regard the knowledge derived from such a relationship as varying in its objective-subjective ratio depending on the point along a continuum at which it is taken, at one end of which we have the sort of relationship which is exemplified in the physical sciences, and then moving along through the biological to the behavioural sciences and eventually to other kinds of knowledge such as aesthetic and religious.

We have seen that even in our search for scientific knowledge we relate ourselves and our intellect to that which we seek to study in nature. We bring to our search for knowledge certain inevitable presuppositions. For example, we *believe* that such knowledge is in fact attainable, that despite the variations in natural events there is an underlying order to be discovered, that there are patterns and regularities if we can but detect them, and that our intellect is such that we are equipped to discover such regularities as there are. This means that we also bring with us the assumption that what happens today in our laboratory will happen again tomorrow if we set up the same conditions. In other words we *believe* certain things about ourselves and about nature, and as we act upon our beliefs about ourselves and about nature we are equipped to embark upon the scientific enterprise. We also *believe* certain things about the skills and beliefs of our fellow-scientists, that they also, if they undertake similar sorts of experiments under similar conditions, will achieve similar results and report them with honesty and integrity. Arising out of this sort of activity we find that there is a very strong consensus of scientific opinion amongst those who are engaged in research in the same discipline, using similar sorts of equipment, in laboratories throughout the world. And, as we have said, it is this intersubjective verifiability which gives to scientific knowledge its relative objectivity.

Intersubjective verifiability and Christian commitment

The relative objectivity of scientific knowledge should not distort our judgment so that when we move into other spheres of knowledge, where the same consensus of opinion is no longer present to the same extent, we are tempted to assert that there is no valid knowledge. One such field in which we find reduced consensus of opinion is in artistic or aesthetic appreciation. If one were, for example, to seek the evaluation of a group of observers of a work of art one would perhaps arrive at some sort of consensus of opinion, but not by any means a unanimous one.

This point is brought out very clearly in the changes of styles and customs from generation to generation. There are those who embrace such changes readily, and others who for many years may drag their feet before they fully, if ever, appreciate the new styles. This applies both in art and in music, as we all know from our personal experience. This does not mean that my judgment is any the less valid, just because I and my colleague who does not share my views, having both examined the same data, appreciate it differently, seeing different patterns in it, so that our opinions about the same data differ.

When we consider matters of religious faith, we certainly find that in the Christian faith there are *data* for us to study. Just as there is that which is *given* in nature for our scientific investigation, so there is that which is *given* in history for our religious evaluation. There are, for example, the evidences from the history of the people of Israel, there are the evidences from the records that we have of the life of Christ, His words and His deeds, the impression He made on those who saw and heard Him and the experience of the early church. Added to this there is the chequered history of the church over the last 1,900 years. These are also in a real sense *data*; they are given to us and they are there for us to make sense of and to evaluate. Perhaps here even more than in the sphere of aesthetic knowledge there is room for wide differences of interpretation. In this realm, however, as far as the Christian faith is concerned, there is a new ingredient brought in, one which we are so familiar with in our daily lives that we can easily miss it in the context of religious faith. We refer to the fact that in studying the *data* for religious knowledge we can easily stop short at knowing *about* all the things that happened to Jesus and the things that He said, without ever coming to a *personal knowledge* of Him.

Perhaps we could illustrate this from the experience of experimental psychologists. It is not at all uncommon for them, in the course of their investigations, to use human subjects in their experiments. They may, for example, be interested in recording a variety of psychological and physiological responses that they find in their subjects. They may be interested in their subjects' ability at processing visual information, their short-term memory, their reaction time, or in the electrical activity in their brains as recorded on an EEG, or in a whole range of other variables. It could legitimately be said in one sense that at the end of their experiments they know a great deal about their subjects. And yet it could also be said that they *know* very few of them at all, in any personal way, since this is not an aspect of them which they are normally interested in in their scientific endeavours.

This is not to say that on other occasions it may be quite *inappropriate* to study subjects solely in this way, so that one limits oneself simply to knowing *about* them, instead of opening oneself to the possibility of getting to *know* them personally. There are times when it is proper for one to open oneself to a two-way interaction, to two-way traffic in which the subject of one's studies is met under different circumstances as a friend and responds to one in a personal way. This is certainly true of attempts to get to know the central figure of the Christian faith, Jesus Christ. If I am to move from *knowing about* to *knowing personally*, from *savoir* to *connaître*, from *fides* to *fiducia*, from credence to conviction, from belief about to trust in, then I must open myself to the possibility of two-way traffic leading to personal encounter. This is not to suggest that it is necessary to adopt a *gullible* attitude, but rather to adopt an attitude appropriate to the relationship that I am seeking.

We have now reached a point on the continuum we discussed earlier, which may perhaps be described as heavily subjective, a point in which both the knower and the known are heavily involved in a personal interaction, which is not the case at the other end of the continuum where we are dealing with physical knowledge. This does not mean, however, that there is not the possibility of some sort of consensus of opinion. In fact there is considerable consensus of opinion amongst those who 'profess and call themselves Christians'. They have responded to the knowledge that there is in Christ in the best way that they know, and in doing so they have found that it turns out to be both self-authenticating and self-validating. And in seeking to communicate with each other something of the experience which is theirs they find a considerable measure of agreement amongst themselves. There is in this sense a considerable measure of intersubjective verifiability in matters of the Christian faith as well as in matters of science.

CHAPTER 4

EXPLANATIONS, MODELS, IMAGES & REALITY IN SCIENCE AND RELIGION

THE NATURE OF EXPLANATION IN SCIENCE

THE central question we shall concern ourselves with in this section is 'What do we mean when we say that we give a scientific explanation of an event or a phenomenon?' The importance of this question lies in the fact that there has, from time to time, been considerable confusion about what is meant by 'scientific explanation', not only in the minds of some Christians, but also of some scientists. The former have, for example, at times regarded scientific explanations as being in direct competition with, and therefore as directly threatening, statements which have traditionally been made in religious language about the activity of God. While we shall not at present discuss questions about how to relate scientific and religious statements, we shall in this section seek to make clear what is and what is not being claimed when we say that we can offer a scientific explanation of some event in the natural world.

Some widely-held views

Let us begin by briefly surveying a range of different meanings which have been given by scientists themselves and by philosophers of science to the idea of explanation in science. Some have argued that to explain is logically equivalent to predicting, and nothing more.

Those who take this view argue that the scientist's main objective is to show that an event which he has studied can be subsumed as an instance of a general law, which he can now state. This approach means that any event, whether in the past or in the future, should be deducible from the application of the law to all the relevant information about the conditions existing before the event took place. Other writers on the philosophy of science have challenged this view on the grounds that many theories which are generally accepted as scientific explanations, such as the theory of natural selection, would be held by very few to have been capable of predicting, in this case, the course of evolution. It should also be pointed out that the converse does not automatically apply and that, while an explanation may lead to the prediction of future events, nevertheless prediction may be possible in the absence of explanation. Anderson supplied an instance of this in his conference paper when he wrote,

> 'For example, if a child is born with phenylketonuria we could explain the occurrence in terms of the behaviour of genes and chromosomes, and we can predict within probabilistic limits the chances that the next child born to the same parents will have the same condition. On the other hand, if the child is born with a harelip we can predict with fair accuracy the outcome of the next pregnancy but cannot explain the causes of the defect in a very satisfactory manner.'

Moreover, it is often in our ability to predict future events, in the absence of any real understanding of why we can predict them, that we find a good deal of our motivation for scientific research. On the argument that explanation is logically equivalent to prediction, one could presumably further argue that scientific explanation becomes unnecessary, provided that you can make the necessary prediction without your scientific knowledge. But it would be very difficult to find any scientist who would be content merely to be able to predict, without being also able to understand the mechanisms operative in the events he is predicting.

Usually explanations become really satisfying to a scientist only when they can be shown to be derivable from theories, which not only give some explanation or understanding of the events being studied, but also suggest their applicability to new types of phenomena not as yet understood. Predictive laws alone must always be dissatisfying to the scientist, until such time as he gains insight into the theoretical structures which can account for their consistent success. No doubt it is for this reason that writers such as Toulmin[1] and Hanson[2] have insisted that one of the central aims of the scientific enterprise is not simply to be able to explain isolated phenomena, but rather to gain an increased understanding or intelligibility of the whole pattern of events that are being observed. Toulmin, for example, points out that the ancient Babylonians were able to make precise predictions in astronomical matters, but they had very little understanding of why their predictions turned out to be correct more often than not. Others have argued that the difference between explanation and description is not always clear, and that it may sometimes be the case that an explanation is nothing more than a comprehensive and accurate description of an event. Nevertheless many would feel that the whole point of a good explanation is that it tends to make use of ideas at a different logical level than the event being described and that it therefore includes that which is being explained in a more general and comprehensive system.

The question that we raised a little earlier concerning the nature of scientific explanations really serves to raise the much more general and important question of how we view the relation of scientific statements to the reality which they purport to be concerned with. Beginning with the empiricist tradition of men like Bacon, Hume and Mill and continuing to the present day, there have been those who have placed the most emphasis on the observational side of science. The form in which this view has been presented by the positivists is that scientific explanations, including the concepts and theories that go with them, are really nothing more than concise summaries of the data being studied. Such a view, however, seems difficult to defend, since the whole point of a scientific theory is that it introduces new conceptual terms which are not the same as the observations which they are designed to make sense of. The important thing about a scientific theory, in so far as it constitutes an explanation of the phenomenon being studied, is precisely that it makes use of ideas of a

---

[1] S.Toulmin, *Foresight and Understanding* (Hutchinson, 1961).
[2] N. R. Hanson, *Patterns of Discovery* (CUP, 1965).

different logical level and which have a greater comprehensiveness and generality than the phenomenon being observed.

Another approach stemming from the developments in logical positivism, mainly within British philosophy, which led to linguistic analysis, carried with it a view of scientific language which is often referred to as the instrumentalist view. This particular view is very widely held among philosophers of science today and its main point, as Barbour[3] puts it, is 'that scientific explanations are "maxims or directions for the investigator to find his way about", whereas theories are "techniques for drawing inferences" useful primarily for making predictions'. Barbour's quotations are from Toulmin's book, *The Philosophy of Science*.[4]

On this view explanation is not to be judged by its truth or falsity, but by its usefulness in achieving the goals of 'making accurate predictions',[5] 'of directing further experimentation'[6] and 'of achieving technical control over the environment'.[7] According to this view, scientific laws and theories are invented by the scientist and not discovered as properties of that which is being observed. In practice, however, most scientists do in fact regard the evidence which they gather in their experiments as counting for or against the *validity* of a particular theory, and they are not simply content to regard it as counting for or against the *usefulness* of that theory. It is not at all uncommon for two contradictory theories or explanations both to turn out to be useful in the sense of generating much useful further work, but nevertheless we continue to seek to resolve the conflict regarding which one of these two corresponds most nearly with what is the real situation, in other words which of these is the valid or true explanation.

Some philosophers would take a different view again and regard the explanatory theories that are proposed by scientists as almost entirely structures imposed by the mind upon the chaos of sense data which confronts us and with which we are bombarded from day to day. Such a view as this ends up by neglecting almost entirely the way in which the data guides the scientist in formu-

---

[3] I. G. Barbour, *Issues in Science and Religion* (SCM, 1966).
[4] S. Toulmin, *The Philosophy of Science* (Hutchinson University Library, 1953).
[5] I. G. Barbour, *op. cit.*
[6] *Ibid.*
[7] *Ibid.*, p. 165.

lating his explanations. It is thus the other extreme to the positivist view which we mentioned earlier. While the positivists would stress the controlling aspect of the data so as to neglect the participation of the knower almost entirely, this view so stresses the participation of the knower that it ends up by neglecting almost completely the part played by the regularities in nature which first caught our attention. Finally, there are those who restore the balance somewhat in that they assert that the patterns in the data, while they are to some extent imposed by us, are not solely imposed by us, but originate in part at least in existing objective relationships within nature itself. They would stress that the activities of discovery and exploration on the part of the scientist are just as important as those of invention and theory construction. Such a view as this regards explanatory theories as in essence representations of what is the case in the world around us. This view was developed extensively by the philosopher and mathematician, A. N. Whitehead,[8] in his so-called realist epistemology.

A Christian view of scientific explanation

Our own view was hinted at in the previous chapter when we mentioned that as Christians we are committed to maintain neither an extreme objectivist nor an extreme subjectivist position concerning the nature of our knowledge of the physical world. The biblical view would be that such order and uniformity as we discover in the range and variety of the world around us is a part of God's creation. It has all been determined and is sustained by the activity of God. Moreover we believe that our Christian faith will engender within us the confidence that we are equipped with sensory and intellectual abilities which will enable us, by perceiving and studying the phenomena around us, to acquire the knowledge that we need in order to carry out the cultural charge given to us by God. On this view, man in his scientific activity is engaged in actualizing this knowledge relation, which is potentially given by the creation, and therefore whether he recognizes it or not he is engaged in fulfilling his cultural charge.

According to this view,

[8] A. N. Whitehead, *Science and the Modern World* (CUP, 1926).

'The nature and content of the knowledge relation will be determined by the two poles between which it extends, by the object pole as well as by the subject pole. The possibility of discovering and describing order, uniformity and constant relations within the phenomena, is certainly due to the nature of the object. But it is equally due to the nature of the human intelligence, which enables men to build up a scheme of logically coherent concepts, which are adequately related to the features of the object. This conception means that the objectivist as well as the subjectivist interpretation of physical knowledge have both to be rejected as being tendencies to ignore, or anyhow to minimise, the significance of one of the two poles between which the knowledge extends' (Sizoo).

From this point of view physical knowledge and the theories, laws and explanations which it summarizes, are all found 'to have essentially the character of a qualified relation extending within the created order between the two poles, the intelligent subject, man, on the one hand, and the intelligible phenomena, on the other' (Sizoo). This being so, any view which minimizes either of these two poles to the extent of failing to do it justice would be a distorted view.

From time to time in the course of our scientific activities the emphasis on one or the other of these poles may justly be increased and on the other one decreased. Moreover our experience tells us, and the history of science confirms, that in order to be good scientists we do not need first to decide whether we accept one or other of the various views outlined earlier, do not *need* to decide whether the pattern is in the events or whether it is in our heads. In fact what usually happens is that, first of all, we notice regularities in nature, we collect our data, and then in seeking to make sense of it we develop our law-making, our theorizing and our explanations, all of which must continually be guided by the data. At other times our activity seems to be almost entirely that of sitting back and turning over in our minds the properties of the accumulated data and imposing one or another of a whole variety of possible patterns upon this data, in an attempt to see which one best makes sense of it and best fits with our other knowledge acquired up to this point. One thing, however, is certainly clear,

and that is that our explanation of the reality which we are studying is not to be identified with that reality, otherwise it would
imply that as our theories, our laws and our explanations change
with the development of science, so the reality which we are
studying is also changing with it, and this we certainly would
not believe.

In a later section we shall have more to say about how our
explanations are related to the physical world they purport to
explain. Perhaps one general point about all discussions, including
our own, of what we mean by explanation, or law, or a theory in
science, should be made so that once again we do not let reason
sit in judgment on what is the case. While as scientists we can
appreciate the worthwhileness of the activities of the philosophers
of science, and of those who are interested in the logic of the
scientific method, we can nevertheless get along perfectly well
with our scientific activities *without* continually stopping to intro-
spect about what we are doing. Some philosophers and some
scientists, of course, would take a much more extreme view and
would assert, as Schiller has, that, 'Among the obstacles to scientific progress high place must certainly be assigned to the analysis
of scientific procedure which logic has provided . . . it does not try
to describe the methods by which the sciences have actually
advanced, and to extract . . . the rules which might be used to
regulate scientific progress, but has freely rearranged the actual
procedure in accordance with its prejudices, for the order of
discovery there has been substituted an order of proof.'[9] In another
place he has been even more outspoken, when he has written,
'It is not too much to say that the more deference men of science
have paid to logic, the worse it has been for the scientific value
of their reasoning. . . . Fortunately for the world, however, the
great men of science have usually been kept in salutary ignorance
of the logical tradition.'[1] One cannot help wondering whether,
in making his point, Schiller is yet again, though perhaps somewhat exaggeratedly, reminding us of the dangers of allowing
reason to sit in judgment on the facts, instead of allowing facts
to sit in judgment upon reason.

[9] F. C. S. Schiller, 'Scientific Discovery and Logical Proof', in *Studies in the
History and Method of Science,* ed. Charles Singer (Dawson, 1955).
[1] *Ibid.*

LEVELS OF EXPLANATION

Anyone who is at all familiar with the scientific literature report-ing studies of human and animal behaviour is well accustomed to finding a variety of different explanations of the same piece of behaviour, without seeing them necessarily as competitors with each other. For example, if one were studying a simple piece of learning by an animal in a maze, it would be possible to seek to explain the animal's behaviour in terms of psychological concepts such as the amount of reward or reinforcement of the behaviour, the intervals between the reinforcements, how many times the animal has been reinforced, and various other similar concepts. It would be equally interesting to study the animal from a differ-ent yet related point of view, namely the changes in the electrical activity in different parts of the animal's brain in the course of learning, the sort of thing which has in fact been done using tele-metry and implanted electrodes. Yet another scientist may well be interested in the changes in the biochemical activity of the brain in the course of such learning. No scientist would think of placing these different levels of explanation alongside each other as competitors and using one to rule out the other.

In his conference paper Anderson indicated how this problem has been present for many years in biology, where it is not at all uncommon to find the different kinds of explanation commonly used grouped in terms of *modes* of explanation rather than *levels* of explanation. The distinguished biologist Simpson, for example, has identified three modes of explanation currently used by biolo-gists : first, explanations which are answers to the question 'how?' in terms of the mechanism involved, often labelled as reductionist explanations; second, answers to the question 'what for?', where one is looking for an answer in terms of function, often referred to as compositionist explanations; and third, answers to the question 'how did this come about?', that is to say answers in terms of the history of the organism. Anderson pointed out how,

'The value of the first type, the reductionist explanation, is well illustrated by the recent rapid advances in molecular biology, which have resulted from the analysis of the genetic material of organisms in physico-chemical terms. The influ-ence of biochemical variables upon behaviour, including human behaviour, also under intensive investigation at the present time, is another example of this mode of explanation. Success of methods such as these, however, should not be taken as evidence that all other methods have now become obsolete.'

The second mode of explanation proposed by Simpson includes 'an analysis of the adaptive usefulness of structures and processes, both for the entire organism and for the species to which it belongs. Of particular interest here are the evidences which come up repeatedly of apparently purposeful behaviour displayed by animals' (Anderson). Thorpe[2] has written convincingly of animal behaviour from this point of view. Mayr speaks of these as instances of programmed behaviour, on the basis of analogy with computer programmes. Others have sought to do without this kind of explanation by talking in terms of goal-directed behaviour instead of purposive behaviour. The third type of explanation, labelled historical explanation, is, says Anderson,

'Usually inappropriate concerning strictly physical phenomena, but in biology it is both appropriate and necessary. In genetics for example, it is impossible to understand the present frequency of different genes without considering the forces of natural selection acting upon previous generations. Likewise our recent concern over the effects of radioactive fall-out demonstrates the application of this mode of reasoning with reference to future events in history.'

The point is that any one of these levels or modes of explanation may well be *exhaustive* at that particular level or in that particular mode, but this does not mean that it will be regarded as the only possible or indeed the *exclusive* explanation, which is appropriate to a full account of the phenomenon which is being studied. This is an important point which we must return to in detail later, since it has implications when we seek to relate scientific explanations to explanations which we have given more traditionally in other terms, including religious terms.

Discussing this same question of different levels or modes of explanation in biology, Grene[3] has pointed out that while biology shares with the more exact sciences of physics and chemistry the

---

2 W. H. Thorpe, *Learning and Instinct in Animals* (Methuen, 1956).
3 Marjorie Grene, *The Knower and the Known* (Basic Books, 1966).

basic search for pattern in the events that are being studied, nevertheless it must also add to this if it is to do full justice to the subject-matter of its inquiry. She has written,

> 'Over and above the recognition of abstract patterns characteristic of the sciences of inanimate matter, the practice of biology demands the recognition of individual living things, and analysis in biology is always analysis *within* the context set by the existence of such individual living things. Thus a second kind of aesthetic recognition, the recognition of individuals, adds to the subject matter of biology a logical level missing in the exact sciences, and at the same time limits the range of analysis to the bounds set by the acknowledgment that individual living things exist. *I do not* mean', she writes, 'that at some mysterious point analysis will have to stop, but that an analysis of an organism which analyses the organism *away* would contradict itself by destroying its own subject matter. Nor do I mean that when we recognise individuals we are adding some mysterious vital something that comes from I know not where, but that we *are* affirming the existence of something which is more than a brute fact, in the sense that we acknowledge it as an achievement : as an entity that succeeds or fails relatively to standards which we set for it. It is a good or a bad specimen of something, cepaea nemoralis or spiraea van loutiens. We recognise it as an individual in respect to its trueness to type, no matter how far analysis may proceed this recognition will always be essential. Otherwise we should not know what we were analysing.'[4]

Miss Grene later goes on to point out that even in an area of biology where physical sciences, such as genetics, are increasingly taking over, this point is still important. She refers, of course, to the increasing relevance of biochemistry to the understanding of genetics. She concludes :

> 'As genetical research proceeds, along with specification, the nature of the whole, too, makes itself felt. The parts are the conditions for the whole, which certainly could not exist suspended in some heaven of essences without them; but it is the whole that *explains* the part, not the parts the whole. The whole is the system (the organism) that makes the parts

[4] Marjorie Grene, *op. cit.*, p. 207.

the parts that they are, even though the parts are the conditions (in traditional language, the material causes), for the existence of the whole.'[5]

And later she goes on to assert,

'Biological explanation, however,—and that is my point in reference to genetics—entails the recognition not only of systematic connections—between *such* genes and *such* phenotypes—but of individually existent systems : organisms existing as unitary four-dimensional wholes, as individuals with a life history in a particular portion of space time.'[6]

Where Miss Grene goes on to argue this point in detail and seeks to face the sort of criticisms which could be advanced against her point of view, she finds considerable support in the statement made by the elder statesman of genetics, R. B. Goldschmidt, in his theoretical genetics. She points out that ideally in the exact sciences an explanation provides some sort of formulation, whether a model or a mathematical formulation, from which statements about a certain range of phenomena can be deduced. To quote again from her book,

'From Theory T we can deduce statements of fact A, B, C, D . . . for even though evidence never entails the theory that explains it, the theory once envisaged entails the evidence. What Goldschmidt's statement tells us, however, is that genetical explanation is never wholly of this sort since we must supplement our theory by reference to a fact which we can indeed circumscribe in the language of the theory but could never have predicted from it : the fact of the existence of the organism O, not as an aggregate of any number of genes, but as an integrated whole.'[7]

And later she goes on,

'The geneticist's recognition of a fruit fly stands in a different logical or epistemological relation to the theories of genetics from the relation, say, of the reading of the temperature or pressure of gas to the kinetic theory of gases. For over and above the recognition of pattern implicit in the grasp of data relevant to theories, biology demands the recognition of

[5] *Ibid.*, p. 208.
[6] *Ibid.*
[7] *Ibid.*, p. 209.

individuals, to which as its raison d'être it has continually to return.'[8]

Later on still in answer to the attack that she forsees that this approach smacks of 'teleology' and of 'vitalism', she points out,

'In understanding and explaining organic phenomena we are proceeding in a fashion different from the way in which we proceed when explaining physical phenomena, (so) this suggests also that *what* we are explaining is in fact existentially and historically different.'[9]

And finally she concludes,

'The discontinuity of emergence is not a denial of continuity but its product under certain conditions.'[1]

What are we to conclude from this somewhat extended discussion of a rather specialized topic within biology? First, that none of the various modes of explanation which have been suggested should necessarily be regarded as logical alternatives or competitors with each other. We would also wish to say that neither should any of them be regarded as necessary competitors with the various biblical affirmations which we find concerning creation. Certainly no scientist has a logical basis for insisting that scientific explanations provide grounds for denying the activity of God in sustaining His creation, or disprove His existence. Moreover the consideration of a variety of modes of explanation in biology, as outlined above, should perhaps help us to see the dangers of speaking over-dogmatically, as some non-theists do, about what to give a scientific explanation does and does not imply about other types of explanation.

As we said earlier, from time to time there has been so much confusion about what is meant by a scientific explanation, that in the minds of some Christians such explanation has been regarded as in direct competition with statements which make assertions about the activity of God. The misunderstanding is, moreover, by no means one-sided, because there are also some non-believing scientists who would maintain that to give a scientific explanation of a phenomenon thereby precludes the

[8] *Ibid.*, p. 210.
[9] *Ibid.*, p. 211.
[1] *Ibid.*, p. 212.

appropriateness of any other sort of explanation of the same phenomenon. To be sure the Bible does contain elements of description, of explanation and of prediction, and it will be our task in the following sections to try to see how we should relate these to the other types of explanation we have been discussing so far, which are given by scientists in their various disciplines.

Relating explanations, models and reality in science and religion

So far we have explored a variety of ways in which the notion of explanation is used within science itself. We have seen, among other things, that there may be a whole cluster of possible explanations of a given phenomenon, all equally scientific, yet some will be formulated in macroscopic concepts and others in microscopic concepts. It is also doubtless true that in some instances a higher level macroscopic explanation may ultimately be absorbed completely into or replaced by a lower level microscopic explanation. As we have also indicated, however, and this is particularly the case in biology, this need not necessarily be so. The question now, however, is this. Granted that we may categorize all this wide variety of scientific explanations together as one group or type of explanation, namely the scientific, how are we to relate this type of explanation to the other type of explanation which has traditionally been given in religious terms? Is there any sense, for example, in which scientific and biblical explanations must necessarily compete for our allegiance and acceptance?

First, we can note that there are several possible ways of approaching this problem which for a Christian are not permissible. For example, if a scientist is also a Christian he will consistently resist the temptation to seek the easy way out of the question of how to relate scientific and biblical truth by compartmentalizing his life, his experience and his thinking. In other words he feels that he must not seek improperly to insulate his scientific knowledge from his Christian beliefs. Any solution that he may arrive at of relating his scientific knowledge and his Christian beliefs must do full justice to the whole of his experience as a scientist and a Christian. This point perhaps is sometimes not sufficiently recognized by our non-Christian scientific colleagues, who fail to realize that our Christian experience is just as much part of our experience as our experience when taking measurements in our laboratories. We could therefore only ignore our Christian experience by being untrue to ourselves and behaving perpetually like schizophrenics.

One way of relating our scientific knowledge and our Christian beliefs, which had considerable vogue some years ago and still lingers on here and there today, has been dubbed the 'God-of-the-gaps' approach. It could be illustrated with a quotation from a book written by a theologian in the early 1950s entitled *Christian Faith and the Scientific Attitude*. In the course of his discussion he wrote,

> 'I am myself inclined to think that the mystery of God's Providence lies deeper than the eruption into nature of such interferences [he is thinking of the possible control of matter by mind] and I am attracted by the fact that scientific explanations and predictions rest now on "the law of great numbers"; that fundamental physical laws are statistical and not exact in the popular sense. Why this should be so is an interesting matter for speculation. It may provide a sufficient room for manoeuvre beneath the observable, regular processes, for the personal care of God to be actively exercised.'[2]

Perhaps the key phrase here is *room to manoeuvre*, which gives the suggestion that nature has things more or less tied up, but that here and there there may be a few gaps in which God can still have His own way. And it is not only the theologians who at times have written in this way; so also have some distinguished scientists, such as a leading astrophysicist who wrote not many years ago approvingly of 'the notion of God continually intervening, with deft touches now here, now there, to direct the material particles in the universe so as to conform to rationally deduced laws'.[3]

Once again, we have the idea of God intervening from time to time in the gaps in the otherwise orderly running of the universe to bring about His divine purposes. According to this view you seek to explain things scientifically as far as you can, and then you bring in God to explain what is still inexplicable at

[2] W. A. Whitehouse, *Christian Faith and the Scientific Attitude* (Oliver and Boyd, 1952), p. 121.
[3] E. A. Milne, *Modern Cosmology and the Christian Idea of God* (OUP, 1952), p. 156.

the scientific level. In this way you divide up the territory of investigation into those bits of nature that science can explain and that God cannot touch, and those bits where science has so far failed and perhaps God could be at work. The net result, however, is that God is left with a steadily dwindling territory, liable to further shrinkage with every new scientific discovery. This, of course, is not to suggest that science has as yet covered most of the ground to be covered. Anyone actively engaged in scientific research is all too well aware of the relatively small area so far conquered and the tremendous area still to be explored. The point is that, however imperfectly the scientist understands the processes he studies, it would be advancing a non-Christian idea of God to suggest that God can be seen at work only in the bits of nature that continue to puzzle the scientist.

We have already provided a clue to the sort of answer which we believe does justice both to our Christian belief and to our scientific convictions, when we stressed the importance of the biblical emphasis on the moment-by-moment divine upholding of the universe as we set it out in Chapter 2. Let us look now a little more closely at what this implies for our present problem. Certainly some of the statements that we find in the Bible have direct reference to the natural order, for example our Lord's own words when He said God 'makes his sun rise on the evil and on the good' (Mt. 5 :45), or when He asserted that it is His Father and our Father who feeds the 'birds of the air' (Mt. 6 :26). Neither of these statements implies anything extra to or incompatible with a physical explanation of the movements of the planets or of the way in which birds are fed. What is implied is that when we have finished analysing the movement of the sun or the feeding behaviour of birds in physical terms there remains a fresh sense to be made of the same pattern of events, if we are to do full justice to what is given to us.

Perhaps this may be illustrated by MacKay's story of the two people who were sitting on the edge of a cliff looking out to sea one evening. One of them was not only a physicist, but a very enthusiastic one, who carried with him a good deal of his scientific equipment in the boot of his car. After a while a light was seen to flash on and off out at sea, and our physicist said that given a little time he would be able to give a full account of the wavelength, the emission rate, the frequency and the various other characteristics of the light that was flashing, according to his own approach to the phenomenon. The friend who was with him became increasingly agitated since in the dim distant past he had learned something of the Morse code and he had become aware that the light flashes were also communicating a message. In fact they were saying that the piece of cliff on which the couple were sitting was beginning to crumble and would shortly slide into the sea. The point is that one could reasonably expect the physicist to give a complete and exhaustive description in physical terms of all that was occurring at the light source, and yet this alone would leave out another, and in these circumstances extremely important, aspect of the same phenomenon, namely the purpose of the events which were thus being observed. The meaning and significance in this case were there for those who were able and willing to read it in a different way. The point is that before one too readily sees two assertions about the same phenomenon as being contradictory, one should be sure that they are not in fact logically complementary.

It may be worthwhile to illustrate this point a little more from a series of events which occurred in the history of science over the last hundred years. This is, of course, an illustration drawn from science, and is in no sense taken to prove the necessity for logically complementary accounts to relate religious and scientific statements.

A hundred years ago the orthodox way of picturing light was in terms of waves spreading through space. The evidence for this view was very convincing and it seemed clear that the earlier view of picturing light as a stream of particles was wrong and could be better done without. But then only fifty years ago the situation changed again when it was discovered that, in certain previously unexplored situations, light seemed to behave quite definitely like a hail of tiny particles. Now the question was which was the valid picture, the wave or the particle one. Only after a lot of hard thinking did it become clear that the correct answer was that both pictures could be valid. In fact the two pictures were not rivals, but complementary, and furthermore it became clear that you could never deduce contradictory conclusions by a valid use of both because they represented answers to different kinds of question. Once again we stress that we use this Principle of Complementarity, first enunciated in physics by Neils Bohr, only as an analogy, and not in any sense as a proof of the necessity of complementary Christian and scientific viewpoints. However satisfied we may be that the two pictures are compatible, it is, as we have already said, only the facts of experience that can convince us that both are necessary. We are here dealing with a logical, not a scientific point, but it is one which it seems is open to a very ready abuse and misunderstanding and for this reason we must seek to see clearly the conditions under which it can legitimately be used. Unless we do this it could easily become an escape hatch which we use when we get into a tight corner in discussions concerning the relation of science and faith. MacKay drew attention to this danger when in 1953 he wrote,

> 'Whenever a new concept swims into philosophical ken there is a danger that it will be overworked by the Athenians on the one hand and abused by the Laodiceans on the other. . . . Complementarity is no universal panacea, and it is a relationship that can be predicated of two descriptions only with careful safeguards against admitting nonsense. Indeed the difficult task is not to establish the possibility that two statements are logically complementary, but to find a rigorous way of detecting when they are not. . . .
>
> 'A good deal of consecrated hard work is needed on the part of Christians to develop a more coherent and more biblical picture of the relationship between the two. . . .
>
> 'But if once we recognize that at least most theological categories are not "in the same plane" (in the same logical subspace) as most scientific categories, there is no longer any theological merit in hunting for gaps in the scientific pattern. Gaps there are in plenty. But . . . it would seem to be the Christian's duty to allow—indeed to help—these gaps to fill or widen as they will, in humble and cheerful obedience to the truth as God reveals it through our scientific discipline, believing that to have theological stakes in scientific answers to scientific questions is to err in company with those unbelievers who do the like.'[4]

In a more recent paper he has spelled out in detail some of the conditions under which two or more descriptions may legiti-

[4] D. M. MacKay, *The Christian Graduate*, Vol. VI, 4, p. 163.

mately be called logically complementary. These he says are (1) that they purport to have a common reference, (2) that each is in principle exhaustive (in the sense that none of the entities or events comprising the common reference need be left unaccounted for), yet (3) they make different assertions because (4) the logical preconditions of definition and/or of the use (that is the context in which they are set) of concepts or relationships in each are mutually exclusive, so that the significant aspects referred to in one are necessarily omitted from the other.

MacKay also points out that nothing in the idea of logical complementarity excludes the possibility of a higher mode of representation which could synthesize two or more complementary descriptions; nor is it necessary that one description should be inferrable from the other. The label is useful mainly as a warning not to try to relate such descriptions in the wrong way, by treating them as (a) referring to different things, (b) synonymous, (c) inexhaustive, or (d) contradictory. The somewhat negative point which arises from all this is that before religious and scientific statements are debated as rivals, it is obligatory that we should establish that they are not in fact complementary. It is also of course equally essential to realize and to recognize that proof of complementarity would not establish that either account was true.

The uses of analogies, models and images in scientific and religious thinking compared and contrasted

We have already noted in passing, in our earlier discussions, the dangers of assuming that the particular analogies, models or theories that we use in science can be identified with the reality that they purport to help us to understand. We have also noted that the developments in physics in particular have weaned us from the nineteenth-century idea that science was providing a *literal description* of an objective world. Such a naïve realism is certainly not tenable today. We now realize that our concepts are symbols which help us to deal with certain limited and restricted aspects of phenomena in order to achieve particular and limited purposes. Concepts are not given to us in nature, but they are terms devised and made use of in our human symbol systems. Not only have we realized that our mathematical symbols are *not* the physical world, but also that our mathematical laws do *not* cause the world to revolve. In short, physical laws do not cause physical processes to take place and we must never use the terms cause and effect in science with this connotation. As Wittgenstein put it, 'At the basis of the whole modern view of the world lies the illusion that the so called laws of nature are the explanations of natural phenomena.'

We have seen how the scientist begins by assuming that there is an objective reality which is available for him to study, that there are regularities in the behaviour of this reality which he can observe and record, and that having carried out his observations and done his recording, he may then be in a position to use analogies and models which may help him to understand something of these regularities. An analogy is usually regarded as an observed or suggested similarity between two situations which have some properties, forms or functions in common, but others which are different. Such analogies help us in our scientific inquiry, in that they enable us to extend patterns of relationships, which we have discovered in one area, to other areas and types of experience. An analogy becomes a model in our scientific theorizing when we make use of an analogy from a phenomenon whose laws are already known and extend it in a systematic way to another one which is still under investigation. Our models may be mathematical models, so that there is a formal similarity in the equations representing the two phenomena, or they may be mechanical models such as the billiard-ball model on which the kinetic theory of gases was based.

Frequently in the course of scientific discovery, 'analogies and models' have turned out to be extremely 'fruitful sources of scientific theories'.[5] Dangers arose, however, when failure to realize that models dealt only with selected characters in the new situation resulted in the tendency to 'over extend them by assuming that all characters of the analogy would be present in the new situation'.[6] When used in this way a model could become a hindrance to further development rather than a help. Realization of this danger led some to take an extreme point of view which suggested that models were only 'temporary psychological aids in the formation of theories'.[7] Several writers in this field, including Hesse, Toulmin and Nagel, have underlined the pragmatic value of models by suggesting that if they are good models they suggest further questions, which take us beyond the phenomena with which we began and enable us to formulate hypotheses which may also turn out to be experimentally fruitful.

Most writers on this topic seem to be agreed that the lesson which we should learn from the mistakes made in the nineteenth century, particularly concerning the use of models in physics, is that models must not be interpreted literally. An analogy is never totally identifiable with, nor is it a complete description of, a phenomenon, only a simplified comparison of limited aspects of the phenomenon with some other phenomenon. This has become more and more clear as the applicability of mechanical and visualizable models has decreased, particularly in quantum physics. In this field it is in fact no longer possible to visualize the way the atom is represented by certain wave functions.

In their discussion of the uses of analogies, models and theories in science, the conference members were agreed that if we fail to do justice either to the object which is being studied or to the subject who is doing the studying, we shall distort the true picture of the relation of such analogies, models and theories to the reality which they are explaining. Thus any sort of naïve realism must be rejected, since it fails to do justice to the part that man's intellect plays in the creation of his theories, and it also fails to acknowledge the extremely selective nature of most theorizing. In our desire for an understanding of the physical world we must be careful not to identify any particular model or theory which summarizes our understanding with what is being studied and understood. To so identify the reality that we study with the theoretical framework that we have constructed as an aid to understanding that reality implies that, each time our theories change in the light of new evidence, we can maintain the validity of our first assumption of identity only by suggesting that reality is changing also. In short, we must always be on our guard against identifying the reality that we study with the analogies, models, images and theories which we make use of in summarizing our understanding of the many-sided aspects of that reality.

[7] *Ibid.*

Models, images and reality in religious thinking

As in science, so in religion we find ourselves of necessity using analogies, models, stories, thought-constructs, word pictures of various kinds in order to think about and to communicate ideas about spiritual reality. Just as in science we make use of analogies in order to extend patterns of relationships which we have understood in one context to another area of experience which has similarities with it, so in religion we frequently use analogies in order to interpret our religious experience and to communicate our ideas about God. The Bible is full of analogies, such as the king, the rock, the strong tower, or of light, or power.

Perhaps parables may be regarded as a special form of analogy in which a vivid story taken from everyday life portrays one central truth about some aspect of the relation between man and God. Even this can be distorted if we try to make every aspect of the parable carry a meaning which is symbolic of some aspect of the God-man relationship. In general, it would seem that parables are designed to communicate one main point, as for example when God is compared with a father or with a king.

We also suggested earlier that in science, when a set of analogies is systematically brought together, these analogies may be used to form a single, more comprehensive model. In biblical theology the central model for God is the human person. And yet at once, as in science, we must be careful to ask which aspects of the model we should regard as important and relevant, and which are irrelevant and inapplicable. For example, the model of God as a person does not need to imply that God has hands and feet, even though from time to time we find passages which speak of God in this way, as for example, 'walking in the garden in the cool of the day' (Gn. 3:8). At the same time there are other aspects of personality such as intelligence and purpose which are aspects of the Godhead from which we can learn much. Moreover, we find particular kinds of personality portrayed to us as teaching us about different aspects of the personality of God, for example God as the sovereign Ruler, God as the just Judge, God as the loving Father, and so on. But all of these are for the Christian inadequate by themseves because there is one supreme model of God, one point at which the model and the reality have become one, namely the Person of Christ Himself.

Just as there are dangers in the use of models in science, so there are dangers present in the use of models in religion. One we have already noted is that if we expect so much from a biblical model that we go on to identify it with the reality it seeks to portray, we may produce a form of literalism which is not merely unintelligent but comes close to bibliolatry. Possibly one reason why we have such a wide range and multiplicity of images given us in the Bible is that they will be mutually self-correcting and self-limiting. We find that when they are used together they enable us to build up a sufficient picture of the total reality that the Bible reveals, for the purposes which it sets before us.

There is, however, one very important difference between the models that we use in science and the models that we use in our religious thinking. We have noticed that in science the analogies, the models and the theories are all devised *by us,* even though they are guided by the data which they are used to explain. In the Bible, however, we find the images, the models and the analogies *given to us,* because in this case we could never, *of ourselves,* have arrived at an adequate conception of God and of spiritual reality. Without this revelatory character we would merely end up by making God in our image. As Van de Fliert reminded the conference, the biblical prohibition against making any graven image or any likeness of God (Ex. 20) warns us against idolatry of any kind, including idolatry in the use of any particular model which we have been given for portraying God to us. We are reminded of this in those passages of the Bible which tell us that God's ways are not our ways and His thoughts are not our thoughts (Is. 55). Perhaps the usefulness and at the same time the limitations of models and images in both science and in religion will become clearer if we now compare and contrast their functions in the two fields.

Just as in science we make use of a model to represent our understanding of one aspect of the physical world and are careful always to remember that the model must be distinguished from the real world itself, so in theology we need to remember that models are likewise ways of representing God's relationship to His world and to us His creatures. The models will be given to us in a variety of modes, in poetry, in prophecy, in chronicle, in letter, and they will be given to us to help make sense of historical events from a divine point of view. They will represent to us the relationship between ourselves and God in a variety of ways, portraying God variously as the Father, the Shepherd, or the Judge. Moreover as our models in science have a certain predictive value, so our models in theology produce in us certain expectations. For example, the model of God the Father enables us to say that God will love us and care for us and guide us and lead us and reveal His will to us.

We have also seen that in science from time to time we may hold several competing models each of which claims to handle the same set of data. We then may apply certain procedures to enable us to judge between these models. These include such things as the parsimony of presuppositions that are made, the predictive range of the model, and perhaps the elegance of the model. It seems that the same is true to some extent in this other sphere since it may be possible, if one begins from a non-theistic point of view, to offer an alternative and non-theistic interpretation of any assertion concerning religious experience which has been made from a religious point of view. In this case we cannot collect extra data as in science, in order to resolve the conflicts, unless we are prepared to do so on God's terms. And God's terms are that we must be willing to know and to act upon any further knowledge that He gives to us (Jn. 7 : 17).

We have noted too that in science we frequently start from the raw data and a few hunches and then proceed to build up our own models to take account of the regularities that we observe in the natural order. By contrast in theology we are *given* certain models by God, which claim to be revelatory. These we must always regard as a template against which we must check any modern versions that are designed to fulfil the same function. Thus we may redress our religious ideas in contemporary thought-patterns, but when we have done this we must always check back to ensure that the essential point that is being made in the biblical model is also made in our revised model, and that the truth is not distorted in the process of transposition.

In science we have learned that an object in a given number

of spatial dimensions cannot be fully represented by a model in a space of fewer dimensions. Likewise in theology we find ourselves at times faced with events whose rationale is claimed to lie in eternity—*i.e.* outside our present space-time dimensions; yet these must be handled by the only models available to us which are those within our space-time. It is not surprising therefore that at times such models appear not only incomplete, but also paradoxical. At this point the doctrine of the Person of Christ becomes paramount, for the Christian claim is that in Christ the eternal was 'projected onto' the dimensions of our space and time; Christ is declared to be the only complete and final projection of God the Creator into our world. In Christ we are given the fullest understanding of God and His truths that can be available to us.

Finally, we may note that in science we find it important to make use of a wide range of different models in order to do justice to the many different aspects of physical reality that we wish to study. For example, we do not falsely oppose the organismic and the molecular concepts of a virus, but regard them both as being necessary to a fuller understanding of that which we are studying. So also in theology we remember that we are *given* by revelation a multiplicity of images or models which help us to a fuller understanding of the many-dimensional nature of the divine truth that is portrayed to us, and that help us to circumvent the inadequacies of our earth-bound thought-forms. We realize that we need all of these held in a delicate balance in order to give us as full and adequate a presentation of the theological truths conveyed to us as possible and of the spiritual reality that is being represented.

We have already suggested earlier in this chapter that the models that we may use in science and in theology should not be falsely opposed to one another but that on closer scrutiny we find that they give complementary accounts of different aspects of that which is being observed. For example, we could present a variety of psychological models of what happens when a person is converted and we could present a physiological model of what happens in the person's brain at his time of conversion. And just as we shall not falsely oppose the psychological and physiological accounts of what is happening at the man's conversion, so we shall not falsely oppose the account which we have traditionally given in religious terms of what is happening at a man's conversion with one or other of the various accounts that may be given in scientific terms. In religious terms we shall want to speak of our encounter with God, we shall want to speak of turning away from sin and from idols, and of turning to God, we shall want to speak of repentance and faith, but our account in these terms is not something which has to be *fitted in* to either the psychological or physiological accounts of the same event. Conversion only makes sense at its deepest level if we see it in these terms.

Models and myths

In the light of what we have just said, perhaps as scientists we may be permitted to mention the puzzlement that we find when we try to understand some aspects of the so-called demythologizing movement in some forms of contemporary theology. It would seem that some theologians have argued that the essence of the gospel is being obscured by the mythological language in which it has traditionally been presented, and they claim that realities about God can best be dealt with in this day and age without such aids, since we have now come of age. It seems clear to us, however, that in seeking to express the activity of God in this world and in our own lives in terms which we can understand, we must use models taken from this world, we must make use of images, pictures, parables and stories from the everyday happenings in this world, otherwise it seems that we must say nothing at all. As scientists we have learned how necessary our models, analogies, images and pictures are in assisting our understanding of physical reality and of communicating this understanding to each other. Perhaps we may be forgiven for reminding the theologians that all the time we are making such extensive use of concepts like electrons, waves, genes, species, reflex arcs, nerve nets and so on, without which we should be completely lost both in our understanding and in our communication with each other, we are nevertheless careful not to identify the models with the reality they represent. In other words to understand the 'deeper truth of physical reality' we must make extensive use of this wide range of concepts without identifying them with that reality. One wonders therefore whether some aspects of the demythologizing movements which are being championed today by some theologians may arise from a mistaken understanding of the use of models in science.

A similar point, it seems, should be applied to some of the things that have been said about the use of familiar biblical models in teaching biblical truths to young children. In teaching science we begin with the simpler and more familiar models and then we may progressively replace them with other models as the child's capacity for understanding more complex models grows. None of us thinks that we do any irreparable harm because we seek to match our physical models to the child's cognitive development. It seems difficult therefore to understand why we should do harm, as some tell us that we should, by attempting to match our theological models likewise to the development of the child's cognitive processes. The error, it seems, that we must avoid both in science and in theology is to identify the model with the reality which it expresses. It would seem that one way of avoiding this error is to make use, as the Bible does, of many different images and models in order to increase our understanding of the truth that we seek to convey, be it physical or spiritual. There remains. however, one vital difference between the use of models in science and religion which we must never forget, which is that whereas in science our models and our analogies will, by their very nature, be subject to continual change, in spiritual matters, whilst we may redress our models in more contemporary dress, nevertheless the basic and underlying templates against which these models must always be matched are those which are given to us by God in the Bible, since these are His Self-revelation.

CHAPTER 5

COSMOLOGY, EVOLUTION, AND THE ORIGIN OF LIFE

IN this chapter and the next we shall consider some of the points of contact between science and religion which have been the main issues for debate and discussion in the past, or which we think may become such in the future. This chapter will be devoted to three issues: cosmology, evolution and the origin of life. The space that we shall devote to each reflects the extent to which they have figured in science and religion controversies past and present, rather than the importance which we personally attach to them today. Thus, while we shall devote the major part of this chapter to questions surrounding evolutionary theory and Christian belief, nevertheless, for reasons we shall give later, we do not regard the evolution issue as necessarily presenting serious problems for Christian belief, any more than the other two issues of cosmological theories and theories concerning the origin of life.

COSMOLOGY[8]

If one makes the assumption, which we believe to be a mistake, of supposing that the various statements in the Bible that make reference to heaven, earth, sun, moon, the firmament, *etc.* are intended, when brought together, to provide a physical model of the universe, such a universe would be something like a house, where the earth is the ground floor, and heaven is the first floor.

[8] This section and those that follow on relativity, presuppositions in cosmology, and kinds of cosmology, are an edited account of a paper prepared by Boyd after the conference.

The earth stands on pillars and has foundations, the firmament is solid and acts as a floor for heaven and a ceiling for the earth. It also separates the waters under the heavens from the waters above the heavens. The waters above the heavens would be contained in a kind of cistern in heaven, where they may be released to give rain in due season by the opening and shutting of the windows of heaven. Beneath the firmament God hangs out the sun to rule the day and the moon to rule the night; stars are embedded like jewels in the firmament. But, as we said a moment ago, all this assumes that the Hebrews took the biblical statements to represent the actual physical nature of things. It seems more probable, however, that they took statements such as these only to represent the appearance of things, and not the physical nature of things.

Other people have suggested that because of their concentration on the theological content of these statements, questions such as the ones that we are raising now, about whether these statements were thought to represent the physical nature of things or not, never entered their minds and they therefore never found it necessary to make distinctions of the kind that we have made. Whether that is the case or not, Christendom has not lacked those who have taken the biblical narrative as a textbook for physical cosmology. The attempt of Cosmas in the sixth century makes it clear that, given sufficient ingenuity, it is possible to develop a very elaborate and, no doubt at that time, convincing basis for a particular cosmology based upon selected passages from the Bible. In his case he started from Hebrews 9 : 23,24, which he regarded as giving him authority for an explicit typological argument which could be developed to build a picture of the universe, and he took the Tabernacle as a physical type or a microcosm of the universe as a whole. Granted this presupposition, his superstructure was ingenious indeed, and in its way quite impressive; but it could only remain that way so long as there was lacking any reliable extra-biblical evidence against which to test the truth of such a superstructure.

In later centuries more sophisticated attempts were made along the same line, but now taking into account what was known of the universe. The Ptolemaic universe was endowed with an ecclesiastical appearance, partly on the basis of a book supposedly written by St Paul's convert Dionysius (Acts 17 : 34), which was regarded almost as an apostolic authority, but which we now know was spurious. According to this, the spheres in the Ptolemaic universe were being moved round by intelligences or spirits, which were identified with the various spiritual powers mentioned in the Bible. The celestial heirarchy, on this scheme, consisted of three sets of three orders of spiritual beings : the seraphim, cherubim and thrones; the dominions, powers and empires; and the principalities, archangels and angels. To round off the picture there were the devil's angels who dwelt in hell below the earth. This scheme allowed for great elaboration so that special characters and duties of each order of being could be discussed and debated in great detail, and the scheme as a whole was given added authority when Thomas Aquinas incorporated it into his gigantic intellectual system which sought to take account of theology, philosophy and science.

As we noticed in an earlier chapter, even at that time there were critics who insisted that there was no scriptural warrant for building such an ornate system based, as it was, upon human reason rather upon the facts of nature. It was not long before the accumulation of new astronomical data was to lead Copernicus on several grounds to challenge the Ptolemaic system. To take the heliocentric theory of Copernicus as a representation of the true state of things meant such a revolution in thinking that Osiander, in his Preface to Copernicus's book in 1543, sought to reduce it to a mathematical fiction and a useful calculating device. No doubt he realized that to take it as a representation of the true state of things would mean the renunciation not only of Aristotelian science, but also the whole theological superstructure which had been tied to it. In the course of the dispute, texts from the Bible were widely used as ammunition. Thus texts such as 'Sun, stand thou still' (Jos. 10 : 12), 'The sun rises and the sun goes down' (Ec. 1 : 5), and 'The world is established; it shall never be moved' (Ps. 93 : 1) were held to support the geocentric view.

The occurrence of two new celestial phenomena, the supernova of 1572-73, and the comet of 1577, followed by the observations which Galileo was able to make in 1609 with his newly-built telescope, added fresh support to the heliocentric theory and helped to remove some of the remaining so-called scientific objections. When Galileo saw the craters on the moon, showing that the moon shines only by reflected light, his conclusion was objected to as being contrary to the description of the moon as a great light in Genesis 1 : 16. When Galileo invited his critics to look for themselves, his observations were dismissed as delusions of the devil or productions of the telescope itself, and the critics declared that they had no need to look for themselves, since the earth's centrality and uniqueness was amply supported by Scripture and the teaching of the church.

Opposition began to grow, not only on the basis of texts, but also much more by arguments from philosophical and speculative theology, so that both Roman Catholics and some Protestants held that it vitiated the whole plan of salvation. They raised arguments which one still hears today, such as that, if the earth is not unique, then other planets must also be inhabited. But how can these people have been descended from Adam, and how can they have been redeemed by Christ? Had there been many incarnations and atonements? These were serious theological issues and no doubt were the main reason why Galileo was made to abjure his opinions and why Copernicus's book was put on the Index. It is of interest that this heliocentric theory was still being challenged into the eighteenth century on scientific grounds and towards the end of the nineteenth century on theological grounds. Nevertheless it does seem undeniable that from the start the issue was taken as foreclosed on scriptural and theological grounds by the Roman Church and by some Protestant theologians.

What may we learn from the history of the dispute? First, that the cosmology which regarded the earth as the centre of things was taken to be the physical state of things and it was not appreciated that there could be a distinction between objective and phenomenal descriptions of natural events, that is between what is really the case in a scientific sense and what appears on the surface to be the case when events are taken simply at their face value, as they appear to common sense and are described in everyday language. The statements found in the Bible were therefore assumed always to be objective. Only when men considered the possibility of another cosmology did they begin to see that such a distinction could be meaningful. Empirical investigation eventually compelled the acceptance of a heliocentric cosmology and it began to be seen that the Bible, when read appropriately as a phenomenal account, made sense. This in particular was a natural corollary of the Protestant view of Scripture that it was designed for the edification of the common man.

As one studies the history of the dispute it does seem that arguments from the biblical texts were only a small part of the opposition to new cosmological theories and that the major part came from philosophical arguments and theological doctrines which were tied to particular philosophical bases. Perhaps this should help us to see that we are liable to fall into similar errors today. Certainly we are not free from the temptation to tie our theological views to particular philosophical predilections, nor are we freed from the temptation to rest our case on naïvely pseudoscientific interpretations of certain portions of the Bible. Let us turn now to the contemporary situation where we still find at times earnest debate amongst Christians over the compatability of various modern cosmological theories with the biblical revelation.

If we are to resolve the perplexities that some Christians face in reconciling their faith and modern cosmology we must first try to understand what the cosmologists actually affirm, and what is the presuppositional and observational basis for it. One of the first things to notice is that cosmologists in particular, and physicists in general, do not regard space and time as such distinct entities as our subjective experience of them would suggest. Their interrelation and lack of absoluteness is recognized in the theory of relativity and its associated transformation laws.

Relativity

We must remember that time is just as much part of God's creation, just as *given* as is space. Until the dawn of the present century time was thought of as an unchanging aspect of existence. It was quite unaffected by anything men could do and quite unrelated in its actual flow to either the psychological state of the individual or the place in the universe where its flow was observed. Certain experiments on the speed of light showed up a more complex situation, however. Speed is a quantity relating space and time—the distance in space traversed in unit time—and the experiments showed that the speed of light was always the same whether measured by someone moving in the same direction as the light or in the opposite. A moment's thought will show that this is very strange. It is certainly not the case for the speed of sound or of rifle bullets, for example.

To make sense of this it became necessary to recognize a certain interchangeability between space and time, so that if one observer were to measure the distance and time-interval between two events, the values measured for the same two events by another observer moving with respect to the first would be found to be different. This implies that *simultaneity* is purely relative. I may observe two events as occurring at the same time at two different places in the universe. Another person may observe them as occurring at different times and separated by a different distance. (This is a real difference, not just an apparent difference, owing to the fact that any signal takes a finite time to travel from the event to the observer.)

By saying that space and time are both part of God's creation, we are not saying that they are created *things,* not seeking to reinstate the luminiferous ether, but simply that they are part of the way in which we perceive the relationships between things, and that this spatio-temporal relationship is just as much given of God as are the things themselves. To give space and time a more absolute meaning or some metaphysical character is to use the words outside their scientific sense 'and *ipso facto* to remove the problem from the arena of scientific discussion.

Associated with the unfamiliar ideas about space and time implicit in relativity there is the concept, employed by Einstein, of a universe which though finite is unbounded—just as to a two-dimensional ant the surface of an orange would appear to be finite (of calculable extent) yet without boundary. Einstein's cosmology was not true to the actual mean density of matter in the known universe, but nevertheless the concept of unbounded finitude is an important contribution to cosmological ideas.

Presuppositions in cosmology

We have seen earlier the important role of presuppositions at the basis of all knowledge. Cosmology is an observational, in one sense an historical, rather than experimental science, and its presuppositions are less uniformly held and so less deeply buried in the subconscious than those of many other sciences. Every scientist believes in the uniformity of nature; that is to say he believes that the laws of physics, applicable in one place and time, will apply in another place and time. In particular he believes, and there is no other word for it, that the sun will rise tomorrow, though he cannot prove it, and that kettles will not boil on ice and freeze on the fire, though he cannot prove that either.

Now when one comes to cosmology, this Principle of Uniformity assumes great importance, for we do not know to what extent, if at all, the laws of physics are dependent on the configuration of the universe at any given moment. For example, do we suppose that the velocity of light (or indeed any other important physical constant) is quite independent of the size or age of the universe? Generally speaking the attitude taken by cosmologists is that we must assume more than we have adequate evidence for or else give up cosmology. If, after that, the picture calculated on these assumptions tallies with observation, our belief in the presupposition is strengthened. This, of course, is no different in essence to the attitude taken in every branch of science but confidence about sunrises and kettles is easier because of their frequency. The universe is, for us at any rate, unique.

The two forms of the Principle of Uniformity held by cosmologists are (1) the Narrow Cosmological Principle, which is the belief that there is no preferred place in the universe—no centre—but that the broad features, including the physical laws, are the same from which ever point in the universe the (hypothetical) observer makes his observations; (2) the Wide Cosmological Principle which includes the Narrow but considers the broad features to be the same, not only at every place, but also at all times.

Kinds of cosmology

If one assumes the Wide Cosmological Principle it leads by logic alone to continuous creation, for since, as we shall see, the universe is observed to be expanding, only by continuous introduction of new matter can its mean density be the same at all times. This is not physics. It is more like mathematics or philosophy or aesthetics. Nevertheless if observations could be shown to be consistent with the continuous creation model, most physicists would find the concept acceptable.

Until recently many of those who only accepted the Narrow Cosmological Principle favoured the idea that the universe started as some sort of primordial atom which exploded and that the receding galaxies are the remnants of that vast explosion. In principle it should be possible to decide between these two views by observing the way the galaxies thin out with distance, but the observational problem is immense and there are many complications.

The recent discovery of the quasars, however, has thrown cosmology into such turmoil that it seems best for plain men (including honest physicists!) to wait for the dust to settle. At present there seems to be a swing away from the continuous creation idea towards some sort of oscillatory picture in which the universe is thought of as first contracting and then expanding.

Both the 'big bang' and 'continuous creation' concepts, as well as the more complex oscillatory models, take the 'visible universe' to be finite, but the continuous creation model seems to imply an unobservable infinity beyond the boundary of vision which presumably contains an infinite number of other 'visible (at their centre) universes'.

That the 'visible universe' is finite is strongly suggested by the darkness of the night sky. If one supposes space to be perfectly transparent, and indeed it does appear to be very nearly so in most directions, then an infinity of stars distributed like currants in a bun would necessarily reveal a star ultimately wherever one looked. They would not, of course, all be resolved but every line of sight would ultimately terminate on a star just as every line from the centre must encounter a currant if the bun is large enough. Such a universe would be incredibly bright, looking something like a sphere whose inner surface was like the surface of the sun.

Arguments such as this lead to the idea that the 'visible universe' cannot consist of a uniform population of stars stretching to infinity. That the 'visible universe' is finite is also shown by another related line of evidence. If we look at the light from very distant sources we find it to be reddened. The only satisfactory explanation for this reddening that has been advanced is that these distant galaxies are receding from us at tremendous speed, and the light is suffering a shift to lower frequency analogous to the so-called Doppler shift in the pitch of the whistle of a receding train. The observations are consistent with the speed of recession being proportional to distance and this fixes a radius for the 'visible universe', since no light can reach us from beyond that distance at which the speed of recession is equal to the speed of light. This distance is known as the Hubble radius and has a value of about three thousand million light years.

It is to be noticed that we have been speaking of the 'visible universe'. Physics is concerned with that which is observable, and, strictly speaking, matter beyond the Hubble radius is no concern of physics, but it is impossible completely to shrug off the philosophical or aesthetic considerations involved in the concept of a universe which is infinite although only a finite part of it is in principle open to investigation.

If we return again to the perplexities of Christians we see that modern cosmology recognizes a world of such vastness that even scriptures like Isaiah 40 : 22, 'its inhabitants are like grasshoppers', do not fully convey our insignificance of size. Nevertheless our surprise at finding how small and insignificant on a spatio-temporal scale we are is entirely consistent with the biblical view, 'When I look at thy heavens . . . what is man?' (Ps. 8 : 3,4). To the psalmist our insignificance merely points out God's greatness and grace.

We have seen that through relativity, space and time are so intimately related that to say that the cosmos came into being at a given instant is automatically to adopt a particular spatio-temporal frame of reference—that for which the actual creating at one point was, for that spatial frame, simultaneous with the creating at another point. For a frame of reference travelling with respect to the first, the affirmation of simultaneity would be false.

It would appear, therefore, that to speak of a particular universal moment of creation makes sense for all conceivable frames of reference only if there is also only one spatial point of creation. A creation at a point in time, as the physicist measures time, is necessarily a creation at a point in space. The situation is analogous to the problem of interpreting evenings and mornings in Genesis 1 over the whole of a spherical earth. This kind of thing should make us cautious about interpreting the Bible as saying anything absolute about the time or place (in the physicist's sense) of creation, and should remind us that to make affirmations on theological grounds about a beginning or end of time automatically involves us in an affirmation about the finitude of space (if space and time are used in the sense in which the physicist uses them).

The importance of this lies in the distinction it points to between theological and physical language and between theological and physical descriptions of the same event. We do not necessarily have to deny the one in order to affirm the other when they appear hard to reconcile. When the physicist speaks of creation he means the introduction of something new but not necessarily *ex nihilo*, as for example the creation of positron-electron pairs in the field of a nucleus with the absorption of a gamma ray. In fact, even if the creation appears to be *ex nihilo* as in the old Bondi, Gold and Hoyle continuous creation theory, so entrenched are the physicist's concerns for conservation principles that sooner or later he will probably introduce a 'field' that is thought of as the cause of the creation event.

Perhaps surprisingly, creation is often used in the Bible in the sense of introducing something new rather than in the sense of *ex nihilo*. Indeed, the RSV translation of Hebrews 11:3 reads, 'By faith we understand . . . so that what is seen was made out of things which do not appear' and Psalm 104 depicts the giving of the *present* scene as the creative (Hebrew *bārā'*, as in Genesis 1) activity of God. 'When thou sendest forth thy Spirit, they *are* created; and thou renewest the face of the ground' (Ps. 104:30). On the other hand the Bible insists on God's priorness to the created order, an aspect of creation which is nothing to do with the question of whether time and space are or are not finite or even are or are not bounded from our point of view as physicists. The priority is in God's time-scale.

The old heresy of the eternity of matter is a heresy not because it affirms that there was no time, in the physicist's sense, when matter was not, but because it affirms that matter has the same self-existing character that is God's alone. The Bible insists that

Yahweh—He who is, the I AM—is and there is none beside Him. All else owes its being to Him, is contingent on Him. He creates it not of necessity but of free will to do so. If that which He makes (present imperfect tense, in the physicist's time-scale) appears to be boundless either spatially or temporally, or both, nevertheless God is always utterly other than His creation, its Giver, Originator and Sustainer. His priority is absolute in His eternal time-scale, not to be found or measured from within our relativistic space-time continuum.

EVOLUTION

The longest paper prepared for the conference was a detailed and highly illuminating account by Rhodes of the development of the controversies over evolution. In his paper he attempted to identify, from the vantage-point of hindsight, the main issues underlying the many popular debates on the subject of evolution and Christian belief. The account which follows draws heavily upon Rhodes's paper and where indicated makes liberal use of his material by quoting particularly pertinent passages in his own words.

The publication of the first edition of Charles Darwin's *The Origin of Species* in 1859 can no more be isolated from the stream of nineteenth-century scientific thought than can the emergence of any other scientific theory from the background and atmosphere in which it arose. The joint paper presented by Wallace and Darwin to the Linnaean Society in 1858 was the culmination of a broad trend that had begun almost seventy years before. For the benefit of non-biologists it may be helpful to sketch in the briefest outline the currents of thought which converged and interacted in the first half of the nineteenth century. In so doing we shall pay particular attention to the various attitudes taken by religious people towards these developments within science, to see what lessons we can learn from them.

Towards the end of the previous century James Hutton in 1788 had published his book entitled *Theory of the Earth,* in which he had argued that the history of the earth should be interpreted in the light of processes known from the present. This great principle, known as the Principle of Uniformitarianism, was to supply the key to the unravelling of the past, and while there were certainly those who were to challenge the assertion that present processes were adequate mechanisms for past changes, it was not to be long before Lyell's *Principles* (1830-35) would produce a mass of evidence in support of the adequacy of present processes, acting over an 'indefinite lapse of time' to account for past changes. Soon, moreover, it was seen that the acceptance of uniformity and continuity in the inorganic history of the earth would have implications for the organic. Thus it seemed sensible for Lyell to conclude that the origin of new species may have been a 'natural, in contradistinction to a miraculous process' (*Lyell's Life and Letters,* Volume II, p.5); and there is no doubt that Lyell's *Principles* exercised a profound influence on Darwin. For example, Darwin, we know, wrote to Lyell in 1845 : 'I have long wished not so much for your sake as for my own feelings of honesty, to acknowledge more plainly than by mere reference, how much I geologically owe to you. Those authors, however, who like you educate people's minds as well as teach them special facts can never, I should think, have full justice done except by posterity, for the mind thus insensibly improved can hardly perceive its own upward ascent.'

We should note at once that neither the Principle of Uniformitarianism nor those like Lyell who held it were irreligious. Playfair, one of its principal exponents, was a Presbyterian minister. For Hutton the approach of Uniformitarianism was inspired by his recognition of divine design in nature. Even so there were at hand alternative theories, such as Catastrophism and Diluvialism, which were soon to be regarded as more Christian than Uniformitarianism. Cuvier, building upon his monumental vertebrate studies, accounted for the fossil succession by Catastrophism.

> 'The basis of this "theory"', wrote Rhodes, 'was that the earth had passed through a number of successive catastrophes, of which the flood of Noah was the most recent. Each of these was thought to have destroyed all or most living things, whose remains were entombed in the strata deposited by the catastrophe, to be replaced by a new fauna and flora, which were later destroyed in turn and preserved in the strata of the next revolution.'

Not only did Catastrophism seem to some 'more Christian' than other theories but it also had the advantage of being the theory espoused by the majority of leading geologists at that time. Commenting on this reciprocal influence of a particular scientific theory and currently held Christian beliefs Rhodes wrote,

> 'Catastrophism was embraced by virtually all the established leaders of geological science in early 19th century England, and it came to be regarded as the orthodox Christian position. Not the least reason for this was probably the fact that it gave recognition to the flood of Noah. The Diluvialists, whose champion was Buckland, not only recognised the "Universal Deluge" as the latest catastrophe, but also regarded it as the geological agent responsible for the widespread "diluvial" deposits in Britain and elsewhere, today interpreted as largely glacial in origin. This argument was itself catastrophic, for Buckland argued that "it is utterly impossible to explain the phenomena which I have called Diluvial, by any causes now at present in operation".'

How theological views could influence the arguments advanced in favour of the respective merits of Catastrophism and Uniformitarianism is further illustrated by the following quotation from Rhodes,

> 'Catastrophism implied more than a particular interpretation of the fossil record and the frequent attempt to identify it with the Genesis narrative. Cuvier, and those who followed him, rejected Uniformitarianism partly upon the assertion that present processes were inadequate to account for past earth history : that "none of the agents that she (nature) now employs were sufficient for the production of her ancient works". This assertion not only allowed Catastrophism : it opened the door to miracle (i.e. miracle after the 19th century conception of direct divine interference from outside) and divine intervention at every stage of the past.'

In the face of the seemingly strong grounds in favour of Catastrophism it was, as we noted above, the great contribution of Lyell's *Principles* to produce a mass of evidence in support of the adequacy of present processes, often imperceptibly slow, acting over an 'indefinite lapse of time'. If such were not the case, Lyell argued, the very laws of nature were at stake. In a brilliant analysis of the whole realm of geology, he argued the adequacy of existing processes (and also, less happily, of their uniform intensity and energy in the past). The particular origin of new species was, for Lyell, not explicable in detail, although their extinction could be accounted for by existing causes. He was led to account for the general absence of mammals in pre-Tertiary formations as the result of their non-preservation, arguing the general destruction of recent vertebrate remains as a sound Uniformitarian basis for his interpretation.

As Hooykaas has remarked, it is ironic that the incompleteness of the fossil record should have been used as a corner-stone for Lyell's non-progressive argument, when it later became the basis of the transmutational interpretation of the fossil record. Equally ironic was the later enthusiasm of Uniformitarianists for evolution (involving the ultimate conversion of Lyell himself by the tenth edition of his book in 1868) and the almost total alignment of the Catastrophists against evolution. This serves only to emphasize the absence of any permanent identification of a particular scientific viewpoint or theory with any given metaphysical position.

While it is easy today to criticize the Catastrophists for at times improperly mixing their Christian beliefs and their science, and to decry their naïvety, nevertheless in one major respect their interpretation of the fossil record was more far-sighted than that of their opponents.

> 'They insisted', wrote Rhodes, 'on a progressive development of life on the earth, with the successive creation of molluscs, fish, reptiles and mammals. Opinions varied both as to the number of catastrophes involved, and as to the extent to which they could be correlated with geological periods or eras, but the notion of progression is in one sense closer to the contemporary view of evolutionary palaeontology than the non-progressive replacement views of Lyell.'

Catastrophism and Diluvialism were not the only competitors with Lyell's views. There were other alternatives which Lyell must have considered and rejected for, as Rhodes continued,

> 'Lamarck in 1809 had argued both progression and evolution, but Lyell rejected his views in equally emphatic tones. Lamarck argued that the evolutionary and progressive character of the fossil record could be accounted for partly

by the effects of environmental pressure in use and disuse ("acquired characteristics") and partly by an innate organic tendency towards perfection. One suspects that Lyell's rejection of Lamarck's theory may have been influenced by the extravagance of Lamarck's geological theories, although biologists were no less hostile than geologists.'

But as the century progressed the tide was turning and in informed circles Lyell's views were slowly gaining ground, so much so that in Sedgwick's (1831) presidential address to the Geological Society he could declare,

'Having been myself a believer, and, to the best of my power, a propagator of what I now regard as a philosophic heresy ... I think it right, as one of my last acts before I quit this Chair, thus publicly to read my recantation. We ought, indeed, to have paused before we first adopted the diluvian theory, and referred all our old superficial gravel to the action of the . . . Flood. For of man, and the works of his hands, we have not yet found a single trace among the remnants of the former world entombed in these ancient deposits.'

Even so, for some time yet Lyell was to meet continued criticism by other distinguished geologists such as Whewell. Rhodes gave an example of this when he quoted Whewell's own words in demanding that,

'Mr Lyell should supply us with some mode by which we may pass from a world filled with one kind of animal form, to another, in which they are equally abundant, without perhaps one species in common.'

As Rhodes went on to point out,

'Mr Lyell failed to oblige and Whewell could continue, "We see in the transition from an earth peopled by one set of animals, to the same earth swarming with entirely new forms of organic life, a distinct manifestation of creative power, transcending the known laws of nature: and, it appears to us, that geology has thus lighted a new lamp along the path of natural theology."[9] This was in marked contrast to Whewell's views of the natural world, of which he wrote, "We can perceive that events are brought about not by isolated interpositions of divine power, exerted in

[9] Whewell, Vol. IX (1831), p. 194.

each particular case, but by the establishment of general laws." '1

But if Lyell could not oblige by supplying 'some mode by which we may pass from a world filled with one kind of animal form, to another . . .' there were those who could. Thus Robert Chambers in his *Vestiges of the Natural History of Creation*, which was published in 1844 and written anonymously, suggested that the key to the understanding of the organic world lay in the process of development by which adaptive evolutionary changes had given rise to new species: 'The simplest and the most primitive type . . . gave birth to the type next above it, that this again produced the next higher, and so on . . . ' was the way that he put it. In spite of these views Chambers dissociated himself from Lamarck, whose 'Hypothesis of Organic Process deservedly incurred much ridicule', and Chambers himself remained vague concerning the mechanism of development and also his book contained errors both of detail and of substance.

But it was not the matters of detail that mattered. His general approach was to arouse public interest, both immediate and widespread. There was also to be theological and scientific opposition. For the scientists, Huxley, Lyell and Buckland led the attack in condemning Chambers's book and its thesis. For the general approach, another scientist, Sedgwick, thundered that 'our glorious maidens and matrons may not . . . poison the springs of joyous thought and modest feeling, by listening to the seductions of this author: who . . . asks them again to stretch out their hands and pluck forbidden fruit . . .'. For all this Chambers himself was careful to avoid any direct theological conflict, so much so that he could write, 'The idea of an almighty author becomes irresistible, for the creation of a law for an endless series of phenomena . . . could have no other imaginable source.'2

The storm breaks

The foregoing few paragraphs outlining so sketchily the events leading up to the breaking of the storm over evolution should at least have made it clear that by the time the storm broke evolu-

---

1 Quoted in the Preface to the *Origin*, from the Bridgewater Treatise.
2 Chambers, *Vestiges* (1884), p. 158.

tion was, as we have said earlier, already in the air, and theological issues had already been raised. Indeed it seemed all too easy for particular scientists to invoke theological truths supposedly in support of opposing scientific theories.

There can be no doubt now that the publication of the *Origin of Species* marks a milestone in human thought, and all are agreed that its influence on scientific and non-scientific fields has been pervasive and enduring. As we have already seen, Darwin was not the first to suggest the possibility of evolution, because Lamarck, Chambers and Darwin's own grandfather, among others, had done this before him. The importance of Darwin's work lay in the fact that he presented such a wealth of evidence in support of a possible *mechanism* for evolution that he convinced the scientific world that evolution had taken place. One of the paradoxical things about this, as a number of authors have pointed out, has been that although evolution was gradually accepted largely because Darwin provided an adequate mechanism, nevertheless one general tendency amongst both scientists and non-scientists was for the gradual acceptance of evolution as such, but the rejection of *natural selection* as the mechanism.

At the time of its publication the general reception of the *Origin* was by no means hostile. *The Times* printed a favourable review written by Huxley, *The Morning Post* was not unfavourable, and only *The Daily News* was hostile. In the many weekly and quarterly reviews receptions were mixed. Others such as those in the *Athenaeum, Frasers,* the *Edinburgh,* and the *Quarterly,* written by Samuel Wilberforce, were highly critical.

We must ask ourselves at this point what were the important issues as they were seen at that time? In the first place there was the theory itself. Among the objections raised by those who opposed the theory, there were some who believed that Genesis demanded the special creation of each species; others while ready to accept the derivation of new species by secondary processes were prepared to do so only when special divine intervention was added from time to time; and still others were ready to accept the divinely directed action of natural selection. Each of these three in one way or another demanded either the rejection of the theory or the direct intervention of divine action at particular points.

The second main issue arose when the possible implications of the theory of evolution for questions concerning the nature of man began to be realized. For whether or not one accepted evolution by natural selection for the rest of the organic world, man was still regarded by most writers as a separate problem. There were some who asserted the need for the special creation of man in a general sense, there were others who accepted his physical evolution but regarded his mental attributes as a special creation, and there were still others who accepted both physical and mental evolution but rejected the possibility of spiritual evolution.

In the decade which followed the publication of the *Origin* there developed the gradual acceptance of the wider application of evolution, but in many quarters still was continuing rejection of natural selection as a mechanism whereby it had come about. As Rhodes observed,

> 'It is interesting to speculate at this point as to why the debate which followed the publication of the *Origin* was to become so much deeper and decisive than those that followed the innovations of Copernicus, Galileo, Newton or Hutton. The spontaneous origin of living from non-living matter, without any special creative act of God, had presented no theological problems in pre-Pasteurian times. The idea of evolution was not new. Lyell had demonstrated it in the development of the earth; Kant and Laplace had suggested it in the origin of the solar system. Some of these theories clearly contradicted the generally accepted interpretations of the Genesis narratives of creation, and yet none of them had occasioned a fraction of the outburst that marked the publication of Darwin's book.'

No doubt the essential reason was that, while each of these earlier innovations had aroused violent opposition, they could still be debated at a largely impersonal level, since they were concerned with the impersonal issues of the physical universe and of the earth. Now, however, Lamarck and Chambers had removed the conflict from the inorganic to the organic realm, and Darwin had carried it even further to man himself, to the heart of the religious domain. Now man himself was not only the inventor and practitioner of science, but had become the object of his own analytical studies. At this point it would be natural at once to

enter into a discussion of some of the continuing issues which
have arisen from the impact of evolutionary theory upon Christian
belief, but before we do this we must, for the benefit of the non-
specialist reader, very briefly review the present technical status
of evolutionary theory.

Evolutionary theory

Organic evolution may be defined as the derivation of species
from different pre-existing species by a process of descent with
modification. This descent is usually held to run through the
whole organic world, including man himself. The fossil record
supplies abundant examples which, according to the theory, give
sufficient grounds for accepting the continuity of all forms of life.
Some hold that evolution has been limited to within a family or
order, but we shall here treat it as the view that all forms of life
are related by descent.

Evolutionary theory postulates a mechanism, and natural
selection represents the best available one which has been demon-
strated to be operating in nature, and is accepted by most, but
not all, specialists as an adequate mechanism for the broad pattern
of evolutionary change. One of the major objections, frequently
proposed among non-scientists by those who are reluctant to
accept the theory of evolution, has tended to be the almost impossible level of proof which they require. Certainly today there are
available numbers of fossil sequences which show specific transition, and, with less certainty, generic, family, ordinal and class
transition too, for that matter. But the nature of geological proof
is that of all historical proof : one has to interpret the data. Thus
no-one can prove 'that all camels living today have descended
from ancestors living 500 years ago', but few would doubt it.
Geological evidence of transition may be reasonably regarded as
of a comparable kind. As Rhodes reminded us,

> 'To demand transition in sexually producing members of
> living biotas is even more naïve. The average time involved
> in the development of mammalian species in early tertiary
> times was 500,000 years. The rate of change of any structure
> is almost inconceivably slow. For example, the molars of
> early tertiary horses, increased in diameter at .2 mm every

million years, yet differences of up to 3 mm existed in a
single population.'

Under such conditions the only possible proof becomes palae-
ontological, and it is claimed that the evolutionary theory allows
the construction of a model which accounts for the data of the
fossil record. For all its explanatory power and potential we must
be careful, however, not to suggest that evolutionary theory has
any more permanence or ultimate validity than any other scientific theory. Theories by their nature are expendable; but at the
present time the neo-Darwinian theory, it is argued, accounts
best for the data and does so with greater economy and greater
elegance than any other.

At the conference, Hooykaas, whilst not disagreeing with
Rhodes's evaluation of the present status of evolutionary theory
per se, expressed an uneasiness about the insidious tendency in
scientific circles to develop an attitude of complacency towards
present theory. It is just at this point, argued Hooykaas, that our
commitment to the worthwhileness of the scientific enterprise as
a fully Christian activity must make itself felt. The 'most
economic' and the 'most elegant' theory at present available is
not necessarily the correct one and to suppose that it is is to do a
gross disservice to science, in so far as it may tend to stifle further
research and new theorizing. A Christian who is a scientist must
hold his scientific views because he is convinced they are the ones
best supported by all the available scientific evidence, and not
because he has been bullied into them by a loquacious majority.
To follow the latter course would be to prostitute one's scientific
integrity. A minority is not unreasonable simply because it is a
minority. Indeed it has often been shown in the course of history,
and in particular the history of science, that the majorities were
wrong. Hooykaas[3] has written in another context,

> 'The "majority" is in general the majority of those who
> speak out, but most scientists do not take the trouble to enter
> into this kind of discussion because they are too much
> absorbed in their research. And even this "majority" is not
> always right. There was a time that every "thinking" man

[3] R. Hooykaas, 'Teilhardism, A Pseudo-Scientific Delusion', *Free University
Quarterly,* Vol. IX, 1 (1963), p. 56. See also R. Hooykaas, *Philosophia Libera:
Christian Faith and the Freedom of Science.*

was an Aristotelian, but in the 17th century the scholastics were considered benighted people and cartesianism was the doctrine "generally" accepted. In the 18th century, however, cartesianism was completely out of fashion. Positive science in the mean time went its own way without caring much for the bickerings of the schools of natural philosophy.'

If there were no heretics in science, real thinking would soon stop. For these reasons we must view with deep concern the way in which neo-Darwinian thought is, at times, today taught at the school level onwards, in such a dogmatic and non-scientific way that it suggests that the last word has been spoken and that it has now become in the scientific field the gospel truth. The important point surely is that this theory, like any theory, may be an extremely useful scientific tool even while we continue to be aware that it does not explain everything, and may indeed be misleading in certain respects. We can nevertheless still use it effectively, with appropriate safeguards, acknowledging its extreme usefulness, while continuing to question its omnicompetence.

The problems and issues as evolutionary theory impinges on Christian belief

a. The mechanism of evolutionary change seen as a competitor or alternative to divine purpose. In an earlier chapter we saw how the model that a person holds of the relation of God to His creation has implications which will tend to colour one's views on a whole range of problems where science and faith seem to meet. Here we have an almost classical example of such a problem. At the middle of the nineteenth century the model held by many Christian spokesmen concerning what science had to say about the natural world was that science and the knowledge to which it gives rise proved the existence of God, and that His postulated intervention at various points within the natural order guaranteed His continuing activity. While this was a seemingly comforting position, it was also a dangerous and ultimately an indefensible one, not only because it involved, as Hooykaas has shown, a semi-deistic attitude, but also because it involved a subtle form of double thinking. As Gillespie has remarked with fairness, belief in God was based upon what science had achieved, and belief in His continuous activity on what it had not. Carried to its logical conclusion, the constant demand for divine intervention over against natural law in the physical realm implied the non-divine character of the 'naturally' explicable. And it was the widespread acceptance of just this attitude that was to produce the deepest evolutionary conflict. One by one the gaps where God was supposed to intervene were closed, the natural explanations were supplied, and the hand of God was removed, so it was assumed, from direct intervention in the material world.

'In vain', wrote Rhodes, 'the Christian uniformitarianists argued that design was better shown by law than by interference. It was not that God could be proved to be incompatible with the new world of science. It was rather that He seemed superfluous and unnecessary.'

For,

'Within the framework of the evolutionary process there have been several subsequent tendencies to regard some parts of the mechanism as "natural", but to recognise others as "divine". Sometimes this has involved hypothetical forces such as Bergson's *élan vital* and sometimes observed processes. Smethurst (1955), for example, is a recent advocate of this view. He has written, "The Christian . . . is bound to protest against the idea that a purely mechanistic explanation will cover all the facts", and he continued, "We must maintain that the evidence of purpose or teleology as seen in living organisms can only be fully explained by the recognition of some guiding or rational power or spiritual influence at work in the realm of biology, and that the Christian belief that here also the creative mind of God is to be discerned, directing and controlling the organisation of the living body, is a more reasonable and satisfying explanation than the materialistic or mechanistic one." '[4]

But as David Lack has pointed out, this 'quality of "purposiveness" or "directiveness" has not been precisely defined, and seems incapable of analysis, and it may well mean no more than extreme intricacy, combined with structures and behaviour closely adapted

[4] A. F. Smethurst, *Modern Science and Christian Beliefs* (Nisbet, 1955), pp. 120, 121.

for survival by a natural selection'.[5] Lack then comments further on the views of writers like Smethurst and writes that they

> 'have claimed that this quality of living matter lies outside science, but scientists may reject the intrusion of pseudo-mystical claims into their proper field of observation. Such rejection does not all imply, as is sometimes supposed, that scientists fail to recognize the marvellous organization of the living plant and animal, or that they think this organization has been adequately explained in the known terms of physics and chemistry'.[6]

Rather, as he later comments,

> 'While the matter cannot be proven, nearly all biologists consider that the available evidence favours the view that natural selection has had time enough to produce the major changes of evolution. The difficulty of Smethurst and others is partly due to their considering natural selection a matter of "pure chance".'[7]

We shall take up questions of chance and randomness in our next section. Lack finally concludes, 'Hence the concept of a Life Force or holistic urge, which at best was a term naming what could not be explained, may be rejected as unnecessary and misleading.'[8] By contrast, earlier workers like Hutton had found the efficiency and fitness of existing processes as testifying to the presence, efficacy, design and intelligence in the power that conducts the world. For Hutton the Creator was visualized as being magnified just because of His total, rather than partial, intervention or exclusion from natural processes which He had once originated.

Others, cognizant of evolutionary theory, have attempted to identify particular scientific processes with scriptural counterparts. It should be noted that this kind of so-called scientific exegesis of certain passages of Scripture still flourishes in some informed, but historically neglectful, circles. Thus the hasty grasping of indeterminacy, or the second law of thermodynamics, or other current laws and principles, as theological rainbows and tokens, is, as we

[5] D. Lack, *Evolutionary Theory and Christian Belief* (Methuen, 1961), p. 59.
[6] *Ibid.*, p. 59.
[7] *Ibid.*, p. 60.
[8] *Ibid.*, p. 60.

have suggested in earlier chapters, subject to all the hazards that made seventeenth-century and eighteenth-century apologetic such a two-edged sword. The transformation of Paley's brilliant, though mistaken, *Evidences* from a monument of bold and effective Christian advocacy in the mid-nineteenth century to a skeleton in the ecclesiastical cupboard in the mid-twentieth century, was largely brought about by the acceptance of the implications of the *Origin of Species*.

As we have argued elsewhere in this book, God, to the theist, while being the cause of everything, is in the scientific sense the explanation of nothing. Scientific knowledge in itself no more proves the existence of God than it disproves it. Thus, leaving aside the question of whether Genesis 1 lays down something detailed on the *mechanism* of creation, there is *in principle* no conflict between Christian faith in general and the discovering of a scientific mechanism for creation. When people (both atheists and theists) say that evolution (as a scientific theory) undermines faith they are quite wrong. In principle it cannot do so. This piece of scientific explanation is in principle no more contrary to Christian theism than any other piece of scientific explanation. 'In this sense at least', comments Rhodes, 'Huxley was right. Like all science, evolution had "no more to do with theism than the first book of Euclid has".'[9] When we affirm that God created we do not rule out the possibility that He did it via a natural process.

b. Randomness and the providence of God. Certain aspects of natural selection as the supposed mechanism of evolutionary change have been thought to represent a unique problem for Christian theology. Some have argued that randomness must surely be the direct antithesis of purpose. But randomness is not an inherent property of an object or objects. It implies only a method of selection or occurrence in which all objects or events have an equal chance of selection. Lack has written that,

> 'Darwinism, in the minds of many, eliminated purpose in any form and implied that animal evolution, including that of man, was the result of "blind chance".'[1]

[9] T. H. Huxley, 'On the reception of the Origin of Species', being Chapter 5 in Vol. II of *The Life and Letters of Charles Darwin*, ed. F. Darwin (1887[2]), p. 202.
[1] D. Lack, *op. cit.*, p. 64.

He comments that,

> 'Smethurst supposed that Neo-Darwinians "attribute the results of the evolutionary process entirely to the blind and fortuitous working of natural selection upon variations produced by mechanistic forces".'

'But', he later points out,[2]

> 'The use of such words as "chance", "fortuitous" and "accident" in this context is ambiguous and misleading. T. H. Huxley long ago called this "the most singular of these, perhaps immortal, fallacies" with regard to the theory of evolution (*Life of Darwin*, 1887). As already stressed, mutations are random in relation to the needs of the animal, but natural selection is not. Selection, as the word implies, is the reverse of chance. On a short-term view, the rigour of natural selection is best shown by the relatively uniform appearance of each individual of the same kind of animal, despite the repeated disadvantageous mutations that arise, and also by the speed with which an occasional favourable mutation spreads. On a long-term view, the best evidence that evolution is not random is provided by convergent adaptation, that is, the evolution of different types of animal into similar-looking forms, through their becoming adapted to a similar way of life.'[3]

The dangers of seizing upon one aspect of Darwinism are well illustrated according to Lack, by recalling that,

> 'Darwinism has also been attacked for the opposite reason, that so far from being random, it implies a rigid determinism in the course of evolution. Such fears have been voiced by both Christians and atheists, but the arguments have prevailed among vitalistic rather than materialistic biologists, among those who see a purpose behind evolution rather than among those who see none. This seems logical, since those who deem evolution purposeful cannot admit pure chance.'[4]

Lack later concludes,

> 'The essential point, as I see it, is that while Darwinism

2 *Ibid.*, p. 64.
3 *Ibid.*, pp. 64-65.
4 *Ibid.*, p. 66.

showed animals to have evolved in accordance with natural laws, this observation throws no special light on the question of determinism; hence determinism need not have been made an issue between Darwinists and Christians, and its implications for both sides are highly uncertain.'[5]

There is certainly no necessary logical implication of purposelessness in randomness as such. For, as Rhodes wrote,

'Even in man, a creature upon whom a variety of influences and characters makes random behaviour a comparatively rare event, random behaviour is not necessarily the antithesis of purpose. To take a seemingly trivial example, one hallmark of a good bricklayer is his skill in random selection of bricks from various batches to avoid colour or texture stratification within the finished wall.'

This, of course, as Rhodes pointed out, is not an analogy strictly applicable to the process of mutation, but it does demonstrate that the recognition of ultimate purpose is not necessarily prejudiced by the existence of randomness. The problem is not one of the elimination of randomness, but rather of the recognition of purpose.

The question of how we recognize purpose is itself a difficult one. The sort of purpose which we look for is inevitably one sought in terms of human purpose. Since at times we find this so difficult to detect at the human level, how are we to determine superhuman purpose if it exists? And then again, even the appearance of randomness judged by human standards need not necessarily be antithetical to superhuman purpose, for the recognition of purpose depends on the point of observation. Can a fly, for example, crawling over a pane of glass in the United Nations building, detect purpose in the structure as a whole? Even if it could possibly apprehend the interrelationship of glass and steel and concrete, could it ever determine the 'purpose' for and within which the building exists? Or to follow another picture developed by du Nuoy, consider a minute insect crawling over a perfect mixture of finely-ground white flour and black soot. To us such a mixture would always appear as grey powder, but for the insect there will only be black and white boulders. On this scale of

[5] *Ibid.*, p. 67.

observation grey powder simply does not exist. So also it is entirely possible that, for all our human ingenuity, we may miss whatever superhuman purpose there may be in the universe if we look for it solely from our own given point of view.

It is here that the contention of the Christian would be that we can know something of God's purposes through what He has given to us by revelation. This means that the Christian's belief in purpose is established on grounds of faith, not on grounds of science, and likewise presumably the atheist's belief in 'no purpose' is not to be defended on scientific grounds but is likewise a tenet of his faith, that is of his particular metaphysical assumptions rather than upon physical evidence. This is not to brush aside the teleological argument altogether, nor to deny that there is evidence of design in God's creation; but such design is not merely scientific purposefulness or the fitness of particular structures for biological ends. If we look simply on that level we are back to a picture of God as a mere watch-maker and that is likely to lead us into a deistic or agnostic rather than a theistic or atheistic view of God. On a purely scientific level the facts ask for such a scientific (rather than a theological) explanation and when such an explanation has been supplied or found at present missing, we have still not begun to answer the very different level question of whether there is evidence here for or against the existence of the Christian God who is not merely a scientific force.

c. Problems centring on the Genesis account of creation. In the closing sections of the previous chapter we briefly outlined our approach when trying to understand parts of the Bible which seem to make reference to the natural order. We underlined the need for caution and humility in interpreting these particular passages and the importance of not regarding the Bible as in any sense a textbook of twentieth-century scientific knowledge. The attempt to read and interpret these early chapters of the book of Genesis as if they are modern scientific statements is a classical example of the point of view which we have endeavoured to avoid. The moment these accounts are regarded as scientific, one at once produces a number of statements which do not agree with geological conclusions and are hard to reconcile with one another. Examples of these discrepancies are the appearance of highly

developed terrestrial vegetation on the third day before the crea
tion of sun and moon (Gn. 1 : 11), the appearance of birds (1 : 20,
before terrestrial 'creeping things' (1 : 24), and the appearance of
'great sea monsters' before the 'beasts of the earth' and cattle
(which we take to imply mammals; 1 : 21). There is also the
problem of the apparently quite different sequence of Genesis 2.
While it may be true that there is sufficient elasticity in the original
Hebrew text to remove some of these difficulties, nevertheless the
English reader must find them real difficulties and ones that
continue to exist so long as he persists in reading the text as if it
were a scientific thesis.

Difficulties likewise remain if an extreme literalist view is taken
of these same chapters, for it is not difficult to show that problems arise if such statements are always taken literally, *e.g.* when
comparing Genesis 1–2 : 3 with Genesis 2 : 4 ff. In this regard it is
at times the liberal theologians who are the worst offenders; as
for example, when they take everything literalistically in order
to caricature and bring into disrepute the views of those who
believe that these chapters are divinely inspired and have important truths to teach us. Such an approach does not respect the
way in which language is used. Today, as much as in Moses' day,
most language uses words and phrases without a scientific degree
of definiteness, and includes many different figures of speech.
There is a good deal of evidence to suggest that the style of
Genesis 1 is more poetic than scientific and this must be taken into
account.

Most scientists are not found to be troubled by these so-called
'inaccuracies', because for them it is clear that the Genesis record
was never intended to teach palaeontology or zoology. 'In this
regard', wrote Rhodes, 'Gladstone was right to accuse Huxley of
regarding it as a lecture rather than a sermon.'

Coming to the task of seeking to understand these chapters,
and aided by the specialist knowledge of the Hebrew language
available to the conference participants through Anderson and
Ramm, our appreciation of what these early chapters are saying is
along the following lines. The first chapter may be considered as
a presentation of a majestic account of creation in which we are
given a picture of God, the omnipotent One, expressing His will
so that at His word the worlds are called into being and

ordered aright. From verse 4 of chapter 2 onwards the scene changes somewhat and now we have a complementary description of God as the Yahweh God, presented to enrich the picture of God transcendent given to us in the first chapter. It is here therefore that we find phrases such as 'the Lord God planted a garden'; where we find an account of Adam and Eve 'hearing' the voice of the Lord God 'walking in the garden'.

The supreme value of these chapters lies, then, in these truths that they indubitably teach; for even if we may not be certain quite how far, if at all, these passages are intended to be treated as history in the modern sense, we can still be certain of many great truths that they teach us beyond doubt. (A similar situation obtains about Revelation 20–22.) By these truths we mean, for instance, the amazing way in which we are presented with a finely-balanced picture of the transcendence of God and His immanence. God the Spirit, the First Cause, the transcendent Being, the One who creates the universe but is Himself distinct from the universe, is at the same time presented as One who has a deep personal concern for man, so that this God, who, as we are told elsewhere, dwells in light that no man can approach, nevertheless has a very special interest in man and all that happens to him. In this way these early chapters hold in delicate balance, in a way that has been understandable by primitive man and still remains understandable to modern scientific man, both the transcendence and the immanence of God; God infinitely far away yet ever present; God as Spirit and yet as Person. And the important thing is that none of these truths depends for its continuing validity and its enduring relevance upon any particular theory about the mechanism that may have been at work in God's fulfilling and continuing to fulfil His divine purpose in creation.

The purpose of the Genesis account, as illuminated by the teaching of the New Testament, is not to indicate to us what traces we shall find in the rocks, but rather that everything we find is of His making; that He is behind everything; that He continues to hold the world in being; that He creates life; that He forms man and gives him an exceptional place and condition within creation, and that having made him in His image and likeness He cares for man and continues to care when man has fallen into sin, so that from almost the very beginning we see God's gracious act in redemption taking place. The little scientific know-ledge that man has achieved through scratching the surface of the problem of *how* God has carried out His purposes, important though it is, must shrink into infinitesimal proportions when compared with the majesty of what has been revealed in the early chapters of Genesis. This is one example. The conference had not the time or the technical ability to grapple with many of the exegetical problems of Genesis 1-3.

d. Evolutionism and evolutionary ethics. Several times in our dis-cussion up to this point we have observed in passing that evolu-tionary theory, like any other scientific theory, will be steadily modified in the light of new evidence and may ultimately be rejected in favour of another theory which better fits the scientific evidence to be collected in future years. This simple and unexcit-ing fact, that evolutionary theory like any other theory has no absolute status, has, however, been largely ignored or lost sight of in recent decades not only by some philosophers but perhaps more surprisingly by some scientists. They have elevated evolu-tionary theory to the status of a metaphysical or religious system which has often been referred to as 'evolutionism'. In the light of this it needs to be asserted quite clearly that there is no necessary logical connection between the scientific theory of evolution on the one hand, and any one of the many varieties of evolutionism on the other. Lack of logical connection between evolutionary theory and evolutionism needs to be stated, if only because there are those who propagate and support evolutionism in such a way that they do not distinguish sufficiently often or sufficiently care-fully between evolution as a scientific theory, and evolutionism as a set of beliefs which they hold on other grounds. Indeed some seem quite happy to slur over the transition from the one to the other.

Since evolutionism takes so many different forms it is difficult to characterize it with any precision. At one time it appears as an ethical system, at another as a system of metaphysics, and at yet other times it seems to take on all the fervour of a religious creed with its corresponding pontiffs and acolytes. For example, as Hooykaas[6] has observed,

[6] R. Hooykaas 'Teilhardism, A Pseudo-Scientific Delusion', *Free University Quarterly,* Vol. IX, I, (1963), p. 43.

'Evolutionism in the sense of Teilhard and J. Huxley is not a science, but a humanistic "religion without revelation".'

The underlying presupposition upon which this search for some form of evolutionism is based has been well stated by Simpson in expressing his own conviction, 'that what is ethically right is related in some way to what is materially true'. The most sustained search of evolutionism of this kind has been for a code of evolutionary ethics.

Rhodes summarized the varieties of ethical codes by dividing them into four main types. The first three have been submitted to a detailed analysis by Simpson. The first is based on two suppositions, first that evolution is good, and second that its process is gladiatorial. But, as Simpson points out, it has long since been shown by writers such as T. H. Huxley that it is not necessary to conclude that evolution is good, and secondly that the essence of evolution is not a literal struggle. This means that the two basic presuppositions of this system of evolutionary ethics are untenable, and thus the system remains unproven.

The second type of system tends to be based on the supposition that life, as distinct from evolution, is good; this being so, anything that promotes life is taken to be ethically good. This at once produces what is known as a survival ethic, but this very soon becomes unacceptable because it leads to a number of nonsensical conclusions. To name but one, it leads to the inconsistency that the man who dies for a cause is bad, whatever the cause. Thus, for example, to give one's life in saving a child is reprehensible. Simpson commenting on this and showing its shortcomings has well said that 'survival will have no ethical significance except as man be good or bad by other standards than merely existing'.

A third view which is a modification of this second type of ethical theory has been labelled as an ethic of harmony. This usually asserts that 'the probability of survival of individuals or groups of living things increases with the degree with which they harmoniously adjust themselves to each other and to their environment' (Leake, 1945). On close scrutiny this ethic of harmony has all the drawbacks of the survival ethic and in addition it has a vagueness which is sufficient at times to make it almost meaningless.

Simpson himself rejects these first three types of approach and argues that the search for an ethic has so far been a failure. Yet since there are no ethics but human ethics these must ultimately be derived from human evolution in particular, and not organic evolution in general, as is the case with the three preceding types of ethical systems. Thus he asserts, 'As a first proposition of evolutionary ethics derived from specifically human evolution, it is submitted that promotion of knowledge is essentially good.' But what Simpson does not seem to see clearly is that his system of evolutionary ethics, based on human evolution, comes under the same criticisms as the preceding ones. One wishes to ask why the promotion of knowledge is essentially good. By what standards has Simpson arrived at this conclusion? Certainly it is not logically derivable from evolutionary theory. We conclude therefore that on closer scrutiny all evolutionary ethics are found unsupported and therefore also unacceptable. Standards of goodness presumably are given either largely intuitively, or given by God, or both, and the Christian position is that intuitive systems, unless they are given by God, lead to relativism and error, and that only those which have God as their Author, and are anchored in the teaching of Christ and His disciples, can be taken as reliable guides.

To sum up, then, we have sought to underline the inherent futility of the attempt to create a metaphysical structure of evolutionism based upon a foundation which by its very nature as a scientific theory is destined to be continually changing. That this is too often forgotten today has been emphasized by a discerning biologist, Kerkut, in his book *Implications of Evolution* :[7]

> 'It seems at times as if many of our modern writers on evolution have had their views by some sort of revelation, and they base their opinions on the evolution of life, from the simplest form to the complex, entirely on the nature of specific and intra-specific evolution. . . . The evidence that supports the General Theory of Evolution is not sufficiently strong to allow us to consider it as anything more than a working hypothesis. It is not clear that the changes that bring about speciation are of the same nature as those that brought the development of new phyla. The answer will be found by future experimental work and not by dogmatic assertions

[7] G. A. Kerkut, *Implications of Evolution* (Pergamon, 1960), pp. 155, 157.

that the General Theory of Evolution must be correct because there is nothing else that will satisfactorily take its place.'

This latter point is of especial importance today since we are often told we must accept present evolutionary theory because there is no alternative. It was particularly emphasized by Hooykaas that we must never cease to be critical of current theory, never cease carefully to evaluate its foundations and proofs, or we may be heading for a scientific dark age.

In recent years, discussions of evolutionism and Christianity have taken a new turn with the impact of writers such as Teilhard de Chardin, a professing Christian and a distinguished palaeontologist. Reactions to his views differ widely as was evidenced in the conference discussions. Rhodes wrote,

'I find de Chardin's views, though expressed in the most tortuous language, stimulating and generally helpful, though not particularly novel.'

The weight of opinion at the conference, however, was not sympathetic to de Chardin. Quite apart from the futility of creating a metaphysical structure of evolutionism on a foundation likely by its very nature to be changing continually, we cannot from a theological viewpoint accept the assertion of such evolutionism that man reaches his true dignity and spiritual fulfilment through reaching the summit of an evolutionary process. For Christian theology there is only one such perfect man, Jesus Christ, and any man can attain his true destiny only in and through his relation with this Man, whom God has so highly exalted.

Neither can we accept Teilhard's view that 'in the last century and a half the most prodigious event perhaps ever recorded by History since the step of Reflection is realizing itself : the access for ever of Consciousness to a *scale of new dimensions*; and in consequence the birth of an entirely renewed Universe, without any change of line and feature by the simple transformation of its intimate substance', for here, as Hooykaas points out, 'he becomes so excited about Evolution that he even forgets that according to his Christian belief the greatest event in history is the Incarnation of Christ and not the discovery of Evolution.'[8]

[8] *Ibid.*, p. 34.

We do not doubt for one moment the outstanding personality and nobility of character of Teilhard de Chardin, and of the challenge to our thinking that his views have made, but these things in themselves must never become reasons for uncritically accepting all his views. To believe in only one evolution, 'from the depth of the matter to the highest peaks of the Spirit', is not only pure speculation, but is in effect a kind of pantheism. And it is this sort of evolutionism inherent in the views of Teilhard de Chardin, which, having been embraced by so many, finds men such as Teilhard de Chardin and Julian Huxley as members of what has become essentially the same religious sect. Evolutionism of this kind has done nothing more it would seem, than infuse with new hope and new blood a pessimistic world. The world has become so afraid of the atomic bomb that in desperation it grasps eagerly at this new gospel, which promises that after all there is an optimistic end for all of us without any reference whatever to the gracious activity of God. For such a view, says Hooykaas,[9] ' . . . propounds an optimistic world view, which compensates for the disappointment about the hard reality of life by an apocalyptic vision of a rosy future, allegedly based on a purely scientific foundation. This is perhaps the reason of its rapid spread, for modern Man is willing to swallow any kind of opiate if it is presented to him in the name of Science'.

THE ORIGIN OF LIFE

From time to time Christians have raised questions of the kind, 'What would be the implications for my Christian beliefs *if* the scientists were to contrive life in a test tube?' Those who have given answers to such questions have tended to take sides very strongly one way or the other, but before we attempt even to evaluate the question, let alone answer it, we must first of all spend a little time discussing what we mean by 'life' since, as we shall see, it can have a variety of different meanings. We shall also see that unless we are careful in saying what particular meaning we are giving to this concept, at a particular time, we shall generate unreal and unnecessary conflicts with Christian beliefs. To attempt one concise and comprehensive definition of 'life'

[9] *Ibid.,* p. 1.

would almost certainly finish up by being more misleading than helpful.

The first sort of statement that we must make is that life is clearly not a substance or an ingredient of any kind that we can measure out and then add to an existing system, so as to make it come alive. In general we use the word to describe a state or condition; the state described is a dynamic one and not a static one, and it is one of continuous and co-ordinated activity depending upon a continual supply of energy which is transformed by the life processes and used for definite purposes. As Christians we are fully aware that the word 'life' is used differently in different contexts and means different things depending upon its context. For example, the biological sciences are certainly not concerned with what the Christian calls eternal life, nor did Christ come to bring physical life which mankind already possessed. Malcolm Dixon,[1] Professor of Enzyme Biochemistry in the University of Cambridge, has suggested that we should distinguish three different levels or categories of life in order to keep our thinking on this matter clear. The first one he suggests is material life. This is that kind of life which is studied by scientists such as biochemists and biophysicists, and which he calls the material life or the life of the cell. Life at this level for those who have the eyes to see it is wonderful indeed, but because it is so wonderful it does not mean that it is not still a mechanism. It is matter and the forces involved are chemical and physical. As Dixon puts it, 'I see no need to assume any special forces at work. Life at this level is a matter of chemistry.'

Material life at this level consists of a complex network of chemical reactions or processes by which the materials supplied as foods undergo transformations into other substances needed by the cell. Given such a complete system the biochemist can now see more or less how it continues to work and hand on its life to succeeding generations of cells. At the present time what he cannot see is how such a system could ever originate spontaneously. Dixon quotes one of the greatest biochemists, a President of the Royal Society, who called the origin of life on the earth 'the most improbable event in the history of the universe'. But Dixon also hastens to add that this is not to say that its origin was neces-

[1] M. Dixon, *What is Life?* (IVF, 1959).

sarily a miracle. God said 'let the earth bring forth' living things and the earth brought them forth, possibly by natural processes; and it would still be true to say He made them, just as we can be said to make things, although we may harness forces in nature to operate our tools. Perhaps we should add at this point that because the origin of life on the earth may have been 'the most improbable event in the history of the universe' before man appeared upon the earth, this does not necessarily mean that it remains the most improbable event once man has appeared and has taken part in the understanding and manipulation of the physical universe in which he finds himself. In other words, we must not argue from analogy with the improbability of life arising originally when man was not present on earth, with the probability of man being able to contrive life out of existing materials today.

The next level of life which Dixon distinguishes is what he calls the life of the organism or the life of the body. And he comments that, although this is quite different in nature from the first, nevertheless it is dependent upon the first. The development of life at this level has received concentrated attention by groups of scientists in recent years as they have sought to understand how the form of the body is produced and controlled by the formation of chemical substances by the various groups of cells, substances which control the development of their neighbours; or how a kind of blueprint of the body is carried by the nucleic acids of the cell nucleus, which bear the hereditary characters, so that one kind of cell may develop into a rose and another into a tiger. So far we have distinguished two levels, the level of material life, and the level of organismic life. It is interesting now to consider two other levels of life which it seems possible to distinguish and which may be related in some sense to each other in the same way as these first two have been related to each other.

It is at this point that we move from matters of science to matters of faith. Since we shall have much to say about this in the following chapter when we discuss Christian and scientific approaches to the understanding of man, at this point we will say only that the life of the soul or of the mind, which seem to be synonymous, may reasonably be regarded as viewing from a different aspect the ongoing activity of the human organism. We do not believe that the soul is something which could be found by dissecting the body, but it is rather an attempt to describe at a different level the same ongoing activity of the living organism. In this sense the life of the mind or of the soul is itself a fully natural process. But what of the life of the spirit? The life of the spirit is often spoken of in the Bible as eternal life. This is the life which Christ died and rose again to give mankind, though in those who do not know Him it remains a potentiality rather than an actuality.

We shall argue in the next chapter that one of the most meaningful ways of seeing the life of the mind related to the life of the brain as a physical mechanism, is to see the life of the mind, the psychological life, embodied in the physical activity of the brain. With this in view it seems to us that it does not do violence to what we are taught in the Bible if we conceptualize spiritual life as in some sense embodied in the psychological mechanism of man, or to put it another way, in the life of the mind. It is this spiritual life, however, which it is made quite clear is the supreme gift which God has to give to man. As the Bible puts it, this life is a gift from God: 'The free gift of God is eternal life in Christ Jesus our Lord.'

At this point there is a suggestion which we must be careful to avoid. Psychologists, who concern themselves with life at the level of the mind, have no cause to do battle with the biochemists and physiologists, who study life at a physical level. But neither do they have any cause to do battle with those concerned with life at the level of the spirit. To sum up, as we shall suggest and attempt to support by argument in the following chapter, spiritual life may be thought of in a general way as related to the scientific mechanistic structure of the life of the mind as it is presented to us in psychological theory, in the kind of way that psychological life can be said to be related to the activity of the nerve cells and other physical components of the human organism. What we are saying is that it seems reasonable to suppose that spiritual life in some sense is mediated or expressed by our psychological activity in something of the way that mental life is mediated or expressed by our bodily activity.

Finally, let us face the question, what if scientists do contrive life out of existing materials at their disposal today? What implications will this have for Christian belief? In posing these questions in this way we are by implication indicating that we know of no scientific reason in principle why it should be regarded as impossible. Neither, we may add, do we know of any statement in Scripture which suggests that the creation of life is impossible to man. If scientists do succeed we shall have a much better understanding of the natural processes that were at work when God issued His command, 'Let the earth bring forth'. But there is surely more to it than this, because if and when we reach the point that it is possible to contrive life out of existing materials, we shall all then, Christians and non-Christians alike, be faced with a tremendous challenge as to what use we are to make of this new knowledge. It is impossible fully to comprehend at this stage the implications of such a discovery. Yet one thing is clear. The Christian must be prepared and ready to give a lead in applying his Christian principles and Christian ethics and moral standards to the use that is made of such knowledge. Faced with such a discovery one wonders how the shifting sands of evolutionary ethics will be equipped to face the challenges and problems that arise.

In conclusion we should note that whether we are likely to contrive life out of existing materials or not is still an open question scientifically. There are well-informed scientists who believe it is highly unlikely; there are others who believe it is only a matter of time. It may be that God intends to allow men to be responsible for imitating His activity in bringing life into existence as He has allowed us to be responsible for imitating some of His other activities (*e.g.* creating very small heavenly bodies and breeding new kinds of plants and animals). The important thing is that the present gap in our scientific knowledge must not be allowed to become a trap into which Christians fall by making use of it as a refuge, or even a citadel, where they insist 'here God acts', with the implication that He is not acting equally at all times and in all places upholding His creation. In other words, we must be careful to avoid letting this present gap in our knowledge become yet another opportunity for resurrecting the God of the gaps.

CHAPTER 6

PSYCHOLOGY, SOCIOLOGY AND CYBERNETICS

'WHAT is man that thou art mindful of him?' This question asked rhetorically so long ago by the psalmist well expresses man's insatiable curiosity about himself and his nature. More recently this curiosity has stimulated him to undertake systematic scientific research in an effort to understand more fully the hitherto mysterious aspects of his own nature. It is not surprising perhaps that it is over issues concerning himself that man becomes most sensitive, since it is all too easy to misconstrue some of the things said by scientists about man so that they seem to become threats to his pride and self esteem. Perhaps it is for this reason that it is rather more difficult to 'sit down quietly before the facts' about man's own nature than about the rest of creation.

The past half-century has certainly witnessed the rapid, at times almost explosive, development of three major new sciences, psychology, sociology, and cybernetics. The newness, it should be said, lies in the scientific manner the disciplines have developed, rather than in the disciplines *per se,* since each has existed in a less developed, less empirical and less exact form for varying periods. Indicative of the rapid development in one of these disciplines we can cite the statistical calculation performed by Professor Boring of Harvard a few years ago, which led him to conclude that if the rate of increase in the number of psychologists in the second half of the twentieth century was the same as the rate of increase in the first half, then by the year 2000 every other person living would be a psychologist. This somewhat terrifying prospect should be sufficient to indicate how rapidly psychology has been growing, and the same is true to a lesser extent of sociology. Most recently of all, and especially since the early 1940s, there has blossomed out the whole new discipline of cybernetics, with its corresponding developments in computer technology. Each of these disciplines in varying ways has raised with a fresh urgency perennial questions about the nature of man, questions such as whether he is free to choose, and if so to what extent he is free. These questions have become all the more urgent since so much more is now known about the biological and cultural determination of behaviour, and since so many aspects of man's behaviour can now be simulated with computers. As a consequence the questions are often asked, is man a mere machine or is he something more, and in what sense does man have a freedom of choice or is his sense of freedom only a comforting illusion?

It seems that some of the unease experienced and expressed by some Christians concerning the possible impact of these three disciplines upon Christian belief arises when they read scientific accounts of the behaviour of man, including his religious behaviour, which omit, they find, all references to theological categories. We may take as our example the case of psychology, since the answer that we give for that discipline will apply also in the case of sociology and cybernetics. One question that is often asked is, How do we relate statements about man in the language of scientific psychology with statements in everyday common-sense language and with statements in biblical or theological language? Before attempting to answer this we should note in passing that the question we raised a moment ago concerning the problem of man's freedom of choice is not a specifically Christian problem. This problem is just as much a key issue for the humanist, the agnostic and the materialist scientist, since all have an equal stake in the reality of freedom of choice and of individual responsibility. Another problem soon arises when scientific accounts of the behaviour of man (or in the case of sociology of groups of men) are presented in terms of cause-and-effect chains of events which are regarded as deterministic. The question then arises whether this means that man is merely at the mercy of internal and external forces and has no freedom to determine his own destiny. Once again this is as much a question for the thoughtful non-Christian, as for the Christian.

THE LANGUAGES OF PSYCHOLOGY AND RELIGION[2]

There is little doubt that a good deal of the supposed conflict between psychology and Christian belief arises because everyone considers himself, at least in a limited sense, to be an amateur psychologist. This state of affairs does not apply so readily in other fields such as biochemistry or theoretical physics, since it is at once apparent from studying the literature in these fields that the terms that are used and the concepts that are manipulated are quite different from those met with in everyday discourse. This, however, is not the case with certain psychological writings. Contemporary psychology covers such a vast range of research and tackles such a variety of problems that, while some of it is just as clearly unrelated to everyday discourse as the most abstruse papers in theoretical physics, nevertheless there are also writings in psychology which look very much like the sort of things which are said in everyday discourse. The fact that many people feel themselves to be amateur psychologists is, of course, quite understandable, since most of us from time to time reflect upon our own behaviour and that of our friends, and in a rough and ready sort of way we work out why we or our friends do this or that, in such and such circumstances.

What is not by any means so widely appreciated is that when a word is taken over from the everyday language of the market place into the specialized vocabulary of a scientific discipline, its meaning may change markedly. Indeed, if the word is to be of any use for scientific theory-making, it must inevitably undergo a marked restriction in meaning and must take on a limited and clearly defined usage which obeys certain agreed rules. To construct a theory is in part to make a new way of talking about certain facts. Once one agrees, as a method of procedure, to pay attention only to certain features of a total situation and to ignore all others, and decides to categorize the data in a particular way, one inevitably produces a restricted language in which words are used each with its own precise and limited scientific meaning. Consequently in psychology one finds terms like 'drive level', 'anxiety state' and 'guilt' being used in ways which cannot be

---

[2] In this and the following section I am drawing largely on my published paper, *Scientific Psychology and Christian Belief* (IVF, 1967), pp. 5-15.

understood outside their proper psychological contexts of appropriate experiment and theory.

Consider, for example, the two quite different ways in which the word 'guilt' is used by psychologists and theologians. When a psychotherapist speaks about 'guilt', he almost always uses it as short for 'guilt-feeling', that is to designate a psychological state or event. The theologian, on the other hand, refers not to a feeling, but to an objective ethical or forensic relation between a man and God (or between one man and another). Not only is it not the same thing to *feel* guilty and to *be* guilty, but the two do not even necessarily exist in direct proportion. When these two different meanings of the word 'guilt' are confused, needless and groundless conflict is invariably generated.

This simple and unexciting linguistic fact, that the concepts of theology cannot be expressed, for example, in the language of learning theory or of psycho-analysis, has not only misled some psychologists into thinking that they have overthrown theology, but has at times made theologians either suspicious of, or even hostile towards, the activities and statements of psychologists.

What is not always appreciated is that once you have accepted a particular brand of technical sub-language, which we may call 'psychologese', you are thereby predisposed to come to certain conclusions and prevented from arriving at others. In practice contemporary psychology makes use of several such technical sub-languages and it is a matter of considerable debate amongst psychologists themselves as to how some of these are related. One thing is clear, however; having thus sterilized a language for scientific purposes we ought not to be surprised to find that at times we want to say things which we cannot say with the tools it provides. Nor should we draw any earth-shaking, or for that matter faith-shaking, conclusions from this fact. That a concept cannot be expressed within an impoverished language is one thing; that statements in a wider language must therefore contradict any true statements in the impoverished language is another, and it is one which does not follow.

PSYCHOLOGICAL ACCOUNTS OF
RELIGIOUS BEHAVIOUR

Should psychologists study religious behaviour?

The question is often asked whether the fact that it is possible to give psychological explanations of religious behaviour means that our belief in God is thereby shown to be illusory. Many who raise this question do so as a result of reading a book such as Sargant's *Battle for the Mind*. They are seemingly unaware that over the years there has been a steady succession of attempts by psychologists to study religious behaviour empirically. In the last few years the Roman Catholic Church in particular has been very active in promoting and carrying out empirical studies of the psychology of religion, drawing mainly upon clinical material and the results of surveys, questionnaires, church records, *etc.* Certainly if psychology is defined as the scientific study of behaviour, then presumably religious behaviour is a legitimate field for the psychologists' efforts. Even so there have been some well-meaning people who have felt that it is profane to suggest that religious behaviour can or should be studied scientifically.

What has not always been fully realized is that, if it is to be regarded as something more than one man's personal opinion, any psychological theory claiming to account for religious behaviour must meet the usual criterion of being capable of verification or otherwise against empirical findings. In practice it is notoriously difficult to study religious behaviour experimentally, or even empirically, and to obtain clear-cut results. The complexity of the subject of study is such that, in general, one must lean heavily upon statistical data gathered from surveys, questionnaires, personality inventories and a variety of other psychometric measures supplemented by case-history materials, church records, *etc.*

Psychological and religious accounts of conversion

Since in this discussion our primary task is to know how to evaluate psychological accounts of religious behaviour, and how to relate them to other accounts of the same behaviour given in other, for example theological, language, we shall confine our attempts, by way of illustration, to a consideration of only one fundamental type of religious experience and behaviour, namely conversion.

The word 'conversion' is used, of course, in a variety of ways depending upon its context. Thus we speak of a conversion from one currency into another, conversion from Buddhism to Hinduism, from Christianity to Communism, or, as in the Bible, of 'turning from idols to God' (cf. 1 Thes. 1 :9). The underlying idea of these various meanings is a change from one state or commitment to another state or commitment. Certainly when used in the theological context the word 'conversion' must be distinguished from 'regeneration'. Regeneration refers specifically to the work of God the Holy Spirit in imparting new life in Christ. A man may profess conversion without being regenerate, although in general we tend to make the charitable assumption that the latter has accompanied the former.

In writing thus about Christian conversion we are merely stating the generally-accepted belief that conversion is an outcome of the activity of the Holy Spirit, in which men turn to God from any thing, or any ideology, to which they have previously given their commitment. In saying this, however, we must be careful not to set up a false dichotomy which could suggest that God does not act in and through every part of a man's life and environment.

While there are, no doubt, as many different conversion experiences as there are different converted people, nevertheless it remains reasonable to ask whether, as we study the reports of a large number of conversions, there are any recurring features which are common to them all or which seem to divide them naturally into certain sub-groups. Over the years psychologists have developed methods of increasing sophistication for the gathering and evaluating of information from questionnaires, surveys, structured and unstructured interviews, case histories, church records and so on. It is not surprising that from decade to decade, from culture to culture, from one form of church organization to another, the results of such investigations vary within fairly wide limits.

By way of illustration we may consider one very broad generalization about religious behaviour amply supported by the results of many surveys carried out over the past eighty years, which is that in western societies the majority of religious conversions occur around the ages of fifteen to sixteen years. Such a broad generalization of course ignores minor variations in particular parts of the world occurring during this period. For example, it is claimed that there has been a tendency for this age to move upwards in the last fifteen years in Britain. Since our present argument is given merely to illustrate the *kinds* of psychological explanations proposed, however, it is not materially altered by such minor fluctuations. Some may prefer to use the word 'decisions' here. If so we should not object. We are merely following the conventional use of the word 'conversion' as it appears in writings on the psychology of religion.

Also, by way of illustration only, we may then go on to ask why, from a psychologist's point of view, this should be the most frequently occurring age for conversion. Several plausible explanations will briefly be considered. According to one theory we could say that around this age young people begin to associate in new social groups which may hold new sets of beliefs. As the forces of social imitation and group pressure are added to those of social learning, so in some instances radical and rapid changes in beliefs are brought about and these we usually describe as conversions. If these changes take place unexpectedly or over a very short period of time, they tend to be classed in the twenty per cent of all conversions which several studies have chosen to classify as sudden. If, on the other hand, the changes have extended over longer periods and do not possess any very dramatic features, then such conversions are included in the remaining eighty per cent of gradual conversions.

There is some evidence that sudden conversions occur most often in young people who have not been members of Sunday school groups. At the same time there is a small group of conversions reported as sudden, but concerning which there are reasons for believing that they are reported in this way because the religious groups in which they occur *require* the reporting of a sudden conversion, since that alone is regarded as acceptable evidence of a genuine conversion.

The most commonly accepted view, then, is that a social learning theory alone can cope fairly adequately in accounting for most gradual conversions. Sudden conversions, especially those occurring in the mid-teens, seem to be better explained by postulating some alternative or additional mechanism such as group pressure or accelerated psycho-sexual development. In addition there is the more widely-known view of Sigmund Freud, according to which God has the function of a substitute father-figure. According to this view, young people in western societies around the ages of fifteen to sixteen years feel that they must begin to assert their independence of their earthly father. At the same time they continue to feel a need for an authoritative figure who can provide security, love, care and protection. The problem is solved, so Freud tells us, by such young people projecting the attributes of an earthly father on to an imaginary father-figure called God, who serves the same function. In this way the young person achieves his independence of his earthly parent whilst functionally being given the same security through belief in a God endowed with many of the same attributes as his earthly father.

These examples serve to illustrate the point that it has been possible to propose a variety of plausible explanations of a wide range of religious behaviour and religious experience. Needless to say, at present no one theory or mechanism can account for all the diverse data. And this is not surprising since Catholics, Protestants, revivalists, mystics, old and young are religious and express their religion in ways which are qualitatively very different in terms of the beliefs they profess and the rituals and practices they perform.

So far we have considered some psychological explanations of conversion in terms of concepts and theories employed in the study of social processes and of social learning. We might equally well have considered the biological and biochemical bases of the behaviour occurring at conversion. We do not doubt that eventually, in principle, it would be possible to describe the changes in the chemistry of the brain which accompany the act of conversion. That such a suggestion is not just fanciful imagining is indicated by the accumulating evidence from animal studies of the changes in the biochemistry of the brain which take place in the course of learning. Alternatively, but still at the same level, we could no doubt record the changes in the electrical activity of the brain at the time of conversion.

Must the religious account be excluded?

Our argument is this. We do not see any reason why ultimately we may not be able to give exhaustive accounts of the psycho-physiological changes taking place at conversion in biochemical, physiological and psychological terms. And we do not believe, moreover, that an exhaustive account in terms of biochemistry will do anything to invalidate or make superfluous that which is given in terms of psychological concepts, any more than the various psychophysiological accounts will make superfluous the account that is given in religious terms. Each will be necessary to do full justice to every aspect of the experience being studied.

Now, it is the contention of the Christian that, in order to do full justice to the totality of his experience, he finds it necessary to see and interpret the over-all pattern of his experience not only in biochemical, physiological or psychological terms, but also in religious terms. To be sure, it will always be possible for the non-Christian to say that he finds *that* level of explanation superfluous or *that* kind of interpretation meaningless to him. And no amount of arguing will be able to present him with an incontestable proof, in the scientific sense, that he is wrong, any more than it will be possible to convince the Christian for his part that he is wrong. It is not that the Christian has a special set of sense receptors which he can tune in to the religious wavelength and which is not possessed by the non-Christian. Rather it is that the total flux of events that goes to make up the experience of the Christian makes sense to him at the deepest level only when he sees it and accepts it for what it claims to be, personal dialogue between him and God. It is not that the descriptions in terms of the various restricted categories of the same events have gaps in them. Such descriptions might be in theory complete and perfectly valid as descriptions on the scientific level. The point is that there are other levels. When faced with the phenomenon of man we find that to do justice to it we have to describe it *also* in terms of man in relation to God. To ignore this level would be dishonest once we have seen the significance of man in these terms.

Now in one sense there is nothing new in this at all. At the time that Christ lived and taught on earth, men's reactions to Him differed. Some accepted His testimony and believed Him to be the one He claimed to be, God made man. Others considered He was mad or a fraud. So, for example, we read in the account that John gives of the life of Christ that after Christ had been teaching of His love, as portrayed in the picture of the Good Shepherd, there was a split amongst the bystanders. The record says: 'These words once again caused a split among the Jews. Many of them said, "He is possessed, he is raving. Why listen to him?" Others said, "No one possessed by an evil spirit could speak like this. Could an evil spirit open blind men's eyes?"' (Jn. 10:19-21, NEB). These different reactions came not because some present had religious receptors and others had not, but because the evaluation of the total pattern of events, including Christ's words and actions, made by the two groups was different.

The same, it seems, is true today. Two people may be listening to a sermon and their ability to understand it depends in both instances on similar psychological processes. These include such things as the learning of a language, the ability to think conceptually and in models, the availability of appropriate stored experience of interpersonal relationships giving some knowledge and understanding of the meaning of things like love, trust and so on. When at the end of the sermon we discover that one person has reached the conclusion that the evaluation of his total experience makes most sense if he believes that Jesus Christ was who He claimed to be, while the other is still in doubt and wants to consider the matter further, we do not believe that the psychology of the first man's experience denies the possibility of a natural explanation just because he has become a Christian, whereas the other man's experience is amenable to a natural explanation because he is still uncommitted. To do this would be to forget that God's activity is to be seen not just in occasional unexpected occurrences, but that He is the sustainer of every part of our lives moment by moment, and what matters is what we make of the total flux of events which go to make up our experience. Perhaps too many of us sample God's activity over such short periods that we do not allow ourselves the chance of effectively grasping the meaning of the totality of our experience.

To summarize this part of our discussion, we may say that, as we examine the descriptions and explanations of religious behaviour given by psychologists, we need to be careful to see them, not as competitors with the accounts we have traditionally given in religious language, but rather as the beginnings of a fresh insight into some of the myriads of ways that God has worked and continues to work in bringing about His divine purposes in men. As we grasp this we shall be freed from the constant temptation to inject some reference to the Holy Spirit into our scientific psychological explanations, because we feel that only in this way shall we be doing full justice to our firm conviction that conversion is in the final analysis the work of God. Professor Austin Farrer puts this well in his little book *Saving Belief*[3] where he writes,

> 'Are the psychologists right? Of course they are right, anyhow in what they affirm. The Holy Ghost is not a feeling, or a finite psychological force. He could not conceivably feature in a psychological explanation alongside other forces or components of the human mind. He is God, and God is the universal underlying cause, not any created or particular cause. He does not inject anything into us, called either charity or inspiration. He continues the creation of our being out of its existing materials, and these are earthly enough.'

What we have just written about the relation of the language of personal religion to the language of psychology applies with equal force when we relate sociology and religion. Sociology, concerned as it is with the study of society and the nature of the empirical inter-relationships within society, inevitably studies the social function of religion. But to see this activity of the sociologist as in any sense a threat to Christian faith is to misunderstand the self-appointed sphere of scientific sociology. For a scientist, sociologist, or any other variety, to make assertions about the truth or falsehood of the religious beliefs held by the people he studies acting religiously, is to go outside the field of social science into the field of personal affirmation about his own beliefs. Concerning the transcendental claims of the Christian faith or any other religious faith, sociology *per se* has to remain silent. That does not mean that sociologists in their personal lives must remain silent; what they must seek to do is to honestly and consistently distinguish between assertions based on sociological evidence and personal affirmations of faith or lack of faith.

[3] A. Farrer, *Saving Belief* (Hodder and Stoughton, 1964), p. 12.

As one distinguished sociologist, Weber,[4] has put it,

'One can only demand of the teacher that he have the intellectual integrity to see that it is one thing to state the facts, to determine mathematical or logical relations or the internal structure of cultural values, whilst it is another thing to answer questions of the value of culture and its individual contents and the question of how one should act in the cultural community and in political associations . . . the prophet and the demagogue do not belong on the academic platform.'

Moberg spoke in similar terms at the conference when he said,

'The so-called "anti-Christian bias" in sociology that seems to some to reduce all evidence of the "spiritual" (or the sacred, the holy, the supernatural, etc.) to natural sociological and psychological processes may not be anti-Christian after all. It is necessary in any science to focus upon concepts and phenomena of the particular science and to seek natural sequences of events, causes, etc. This approach becomes anti-Christian only when accompanying interpretations of observable data go beyond the observations, to implications about the absence of supernatural elements in human experience, about God as a figment of the collective imagination, and other scientifically indefensible claims. It would equally seem mistaken in sociology, as in psychology, to look for conclusive scientific proof of the spiritual dimension of human experience, for alternative explanations or interpretations of the alleged evidence are always possible.'

Finally, in this section, what have we to say about the language of the computer technologist who simulates human behaviour on his computer and its relation to the language of personal decision, which we are accustomed to use in our discussions of Christian experience as well as in our day-to-day interpersonal dialogue? Because we can talk about and describe behaviour in terms of brain-talk or artificial brain, *i.e.* computer-talk, does that mean that our familiar talk in terms of personal choices is now irrelevant and redundant?

Since we shall be taking this problem up in greater detail a

---

[4] M. Weber, *Science as a Vocation.*

little later when we discuss determinism, we shall content our-selves now with pointing out that a set of events may demand explanations and descriptions at more than one conceptual level to do full justice to all its aspects. For example, if we write $2 + 2 = 4$ on the blackboard, it would be perfectly reasonable for an analytical chemist to assert that all that is on the board is so much calcium, sulphur, oxygen, and so on. And from his view-point and at that level he would surely be correct. Yet to leave out altogether from a full description of the same phenomenon all reference to the mathematical equation would be to miss the point of what is written on the board. The two levels of descrip-tion are related; they are necessary correlates of one another; but questions asked in the language of the one cannot meaningfully be answered in the language of the other. We have to stick to the conceptual level at which a question is framed in order to find a meaningful answer. Thus, to answer our earlier question, if we are to use language consistently we cannot say that brains (arti-ficial or natural) think or decide or do any such things. It is people who think or decide. Brains and computers do those physical things appropriate in their own logical dimensions as correlates of what people do when deciding, thinking, feeling, believing, and so on.

There remains one further question since Christians assert that there *is* another conceptual level which they find necessary to do full justice to their experience as Christians, namely the spiritual level. How is this related to the other two? MacKay has helpfully suggested that in the same way that psychological life is embodied in the physical structure of the brain (or the equation in the chalk) so we may see spiritual life as 'embodied' in the psycho-logical mechanisms of man. He has written,

> 'I am suggesting, then, that spiritual life may be thought of in a general way as related to the scientific mechanistic structure of psychological theory (with which Freud among others has dealt) in the kind of way that psychological life can be said to be related to the activity of the nerve cells and other mechanical components (with which physiology is concerned). True, as distinct from superficial, conversion is the only way known to Christian faith of bringing about this transformation in a way which "follows on" and does not do

violence to the personality embodied. I can perhaps illustrate what I mean by coming back for a moment to our problem in geometry set out on the blackboard. It could be viewed on the one hand as nothing but chalk, and on the other as a figure of lines and angles. Now the problem can be altered in any number of ways by rearranging the chalk. If we do violence to it as a problem by laying down new lines or rubbing out old lines and changing them, then we get a new problem, or our problem is removed, but we have achieved this only at the cost of *doing violence* to it. The mathematicians are concerned with the only kind of resolution that interests them, namely by discussing the thing at its own level, respecting its nature, and not forcing or distorting it. Similarly, while in principle one might imagine that by suitable surgical manipulations we might turn an angry man into a peaceful man, and so forth, this would not amount to conversion in the biblical sense, for we would have "solved" the man's problem at this level by doing violence to the man. In a sense we would have ended up with a different and a mutilated personality. As I understand the claim of Jesus Christ, that only through Him could eternal life come to us as personalities, it indicates that only by His power as the Creator and Upholder and Redeemer of our whole being can our personality be reshaped in a way that does not do violence to us. Only His way of repentance, forgiveness and love preserves the *continuity* between us as we are now, faced with the problem of our self-centredness and our rebellion against God, and us as we shall be when He has turned our hearts to God.'[5]

Once again therefore we have been warned of the danger of falsely opposing two or more accounts of the same events and thus generating unreal and unnecessary conflicts. At the same time we remind the reader that for the reasons given in detail in the previous chapter we do not believe this is just a convenient refuge whenever an apparent conflict arises. As we have indicated there, there are clear criteria which can and must be applied whenever it is asserted that descriptions at more than one conceptual level are necessary to account fully for a set of events.

[5] D. M. MacKay, ed., *'Christianity in a Mechanistic Universe' and Other Essays* (IVF, 1965), pp. 68, 69.

DETERMINISM IN PSYCHOLOGY, SOCIOLOGY
AND CYBERNETICS

As we consider the specific problem of determinism we should note two things : first, that it is not a new problem but has seemed to become more acute in the light of recent scientific developments, and second, that it is not, as we have already noted, a problem exclusively for the Christian, but it is a problem for all men who take seriously the freedom of mankind to choose and to act responsibly. In the Christian context, however, it is of particular importance because the Christian faith claims that choices made now have implications not only for this life, but for a life beyond this life. This no doubt is why this problem is given an added urgency in the writings of Christian philosophers.

Throughout the biblical narrative we find man as depicted in situations in which he is constantly obliged to choose, to choose between good and evil, to choose between God's way and other ways. We thus find man exhorted, 'Choose this day whom you will serve' (Jos. 24 : 15), and we find Christ Himself issuing an invitation which implies a choice, when He says 'Come to me, all who labour and are heavy-laden, and I will give you rest' (Mt. 11 : 28). And again we are told later in the Bible that 'to all who received him . . . , he gave power to become children of God' (Jn. 1 : 12). These and many other passages all imply a freedom to choose or not to choose, to come or not to come, to follow, or not to follow, to receive or not to receive, to believe or not to believe, to trust or not to trust.

It could be argued, and has been by some, that if there is a problem then it is a problem made by the scientists themselves and one which therefore it is up to them to solve. For example, MacKay, in a recent symposium on brain and conscious experience has written,

> 'Our question . . . is not : can we believe in our freedom on the basis of what we know of physiology, but quite the other way round : Do these facts of our experience create an embarrassment for theoretical physiology?'[6]

Nevertheless the point remains that as scientists we make the

[6] J. C. Eccles, ed., *Brain and Conscious Experience* (Springer-Verlag, 1966), p. 567.

assumption of some form of determinism the basis of our methods of procedure in research; if we did not do this then we should be embarking upon a pointless venture. Some would make the assumption of what may be called a 'strong' determinism, which assumes a fully determinate system and not one determinate within statistical limits; others would assume a form of 'weak' determinism, which is content with determinism within certain statistical limits, so that predictions about behaviour are made on a probabilistic basis only. What has happened, of course, is that the behavioural scientist has made the assumption of some form of determinism in designing his experiments and interpreting his results, and he has found this to be a very effective approach in his research. This sort of determinism is sometimes referred to as methodological determinism, and the success achieved using this approach so far has led some scientists to extend this form of determinism into a general approach to the study of behaviour known as empirical determinism.

What the scientist is saying essentially is that he expects to find regularities in behaviour, as in other natural processes, and that he does not believe that at rock bottom any apparent irregularities are ultimately capricious or unpredictable. As far as this goes there does not seem to be anything which is in obvious conflict with Christian belief. As far as one can see there is nothing in the teaching of the Bible which would lead one to expect that the behaviour of men and animals will not exhibit the order, regularity and lawfulness of the kind we already expect to find in the physical, non-living, parts of the created order. Basically we are all made of the same stuff, of the 'dust of the earth', and Christian teaching does not seem to require us to believe that when this 'stuff' is made up into men it will cease to behave in an orderly and regular fashion. Indeed such clues as there are on this topic in the Bible would incline one to expect lawfulness and predictability in behaviour. The theme that, what a man sows shall he also reap, seems entirely consistent with the belief that what we do and what is done to us today will modify us and thus our behaviour in a determinate manner.

Some sociologists, perhaps over-impressed with the moulding influence of social pressures and social sanctions, have tended to assign to the individual an almost exclusively passive part in the social process. Others, such as Weber, lay greater stress on the role of the individual in influencing social change and it can be fairly stated that few, if any, modern sociologists would be prepared to defend a position which asserts that the individual is a passive victim of social forces wholly outside his control. Nevertheless in the course of the development of any individual it is his culture which not only defines for him what reality is, but also to a large extent defines his goals for him. The fact that this cultural determination is regarded as a problem by some is because it seems hard to reconcile with the doctrine and experience of a sovereign God who is not confined to man's structures. So the question is often put, 'If man's actions and conventions are so determined by his culture, how can one be sure that this God is not also the product of the collective projections of our social environment; and how can one be sure that man's conversion is not just an objectivized wish-dream coming home to roost?'

The answer lies in the fact that, as Mol[7] has written,

> 'Whilst acknowledging that indeed man's aspirations, actions, and also his religion, are to an important extent influenced by his culture, this does not necessarily mean that Christians will have to accept the cultural definitions of their present situation as though they are ultimate reality.'

Moreover, it is an essential component of Christian faith that God has, through the prophets, and pre-eminently in Christ, revealed His divine purposes for man and society. The Christian therefore insists that, bound though he may be to a limited and carefully-defined number of choices, his individual freedom is not derived from greater independence from these choices, but by ensuring that *his* choices are conditioned and directed by what God has revealed about His purposes and plans for mankind and his world. But the question remains, is man free to choose? It is to problems of individual choice behaviour that we must now turn.

Freedom to choose—fact or fiction?

Psychologists of a variety of different persuasions hold a philosophy of determinism in different ways. There are those like B. F. Skinner, a leader amongst the behaviourists, who says, for

---

[7] J. J. Mol, Unpublished paper prepared for the Australian RSCF Conference, 1964, entitled *Sociological Determination and the Christian Man*.

example, 'If we are to use the methods of science in the field of human affairs, we must assume that behaviour is lawful and determined.'[8] Among the more psycho-dynamically orientated psychologists and psychotherapists we could quote Carl Rogers who writes, 'Behaviour when it is examined scientifically, is surely best understood as determined by prior causation. This is one great fact of science.'[9] Having said this, however, we must presumably assume that even those like Skinner do not assume that the kind of determinism which he finds important from a methodological point of view thereby removes any freedom of choice in his own behaviour. Presumably if he is completely determinate, then his own thinking that he is determinate is itself only the result of impersonal factors and is therefore not a meaningful decision. In other words, there will be no external criteria for deciding whether or not Skinner is right or wrong in believing in determinism of a kind which excludes freedom of choice, since his own thinking about determinism is, on his view, itself not open to change in the light of new evidence.

It seems that Carl Rogers has faced this problem, but at the level which is open to all of us, namely our common experience of freedom. He writes, 'That responsible personal choice, which is the core experience of psychotherapy, and which exists prior to any scientific endeavour, is an equally prominent fact in our lives. To deny the experience of responsible choice is as restricted a view as to deny the possibility of behavioural science.'[1] This is the viewpoint also taken by many prominent physiologists, as shown by the published proceedings of the recent symposium on brain and conscious experience referred to above. One participant, emphasizing the primacy of our personal knowledge and experience of what it means to choose freely, wrote, 'My capacity for conscious action, whatever it may mean in mechanical terms, is one of the least dubitable of data, at least for me.'[2]

The point surely is that, if there is a problem, it is a problem for the scientist, since the experience of freedom which is basic

[8] B. F. Skinner, *Science and Human Behaviour* (Macmillan, New York, 1953), p. 6.
[9] C. Rogers and B. F. Skinner, 'Some Issues Concerning the Control of Human Behaviour', *Science*, Vol. CXXIV (1956), p. 1057.
[1] *Ibid.*
[2] J. C. Eccles, ed., *op. cit.*, p. 423.

to our human existence cannot lightly be pushed aside and described as illusory just because a few of us scientists find a particular model of the brain the best that we can come up with at the present time. This being so, one must have a lot of sympathy for those who feel that to devote too much time to the question of determinism and freedom of choice is tilting at a windmill. Since the windmill seems very large and real today, however, and poses a serious problem in many people's minds, it is incumbent upon us to examine it carefully and to see the sorts of answer which have been given to this question. The basic question is usually put something like this : 'If my brain is a physically determinate system, then in what sense can I be said to have any freedom of choice ?' To put this in the Christian context one must ask whether the invitation to choose God's way, to follow Christ or not, is a real invitation or a mere mockery.

One way of cutting the Gordian knot presented by this question has been to take up a dualist position which in essence asserts that there are two kinds of 'stuff', mind and body, and that because the body is determinate it does not therefore mean that the mind is also determinate. Most scientists today, however, would agree that evidence concerning the endogenous and exogenous determinants of behaviour has been accumulating at a steady rate and making more and more implausible this kind of dichotomy between mind 'stuff' and body 'stuff'. Having said this it must be made clear that such a dualist view is held, for example, by some psychologists, often those interested in problems of extra-sensory perception, para-psychology and psychical research. And of course they may turn out to be right. We do not wish in any way to suggest that it is necessary to foreclose such issues, which will demand much more research before we can see more clearly what they imply for our understanding of the nature of man. What we shall argue is that it is not *necessary* to hold a view which implies a dualism of the 'stuff' of which man is made, in order to safeguard freedom of choice.

For the benefit of readers who are not acquainted with the research in this field, we should perhaps just enumerate the sort of research findings which have increased our belief that the mind is not independent of the brain in the way that is suggested in the sort of dualist position which asserts the existence of two different kinds of 'stuff'. In the first place, there is a body of research on animals showing the way in which the steadily-increasing complexity of the nervous system is related to the steadily-increasing repertoire in the behaviour of animals, so that complexity of behaviour closely parallels development of the brain and the nervous system. There is also a mass of evidence from the results of studies on the effects of lesions on the nervous system on psychological functions such as learning, perception, discrimination and memory. Likewise, in those cases where for various reasons the brain fails to develop normally, we find differing kinds of mental abnormality and mental deficiency. Or again, where an adult is afflicted with disease of the brain this frequently is accompanied by the deterioration of mental function. In some behaviour disorders also there is evidence which shows that changes in social and moral behaviour are related to changes in the structure of the brain. The first convincing evidence of this is probably that which came to light following an epidemic of encephalitis lethargica in 1916. It was then noted that some children who had been attacked by this infection, and as a result suffered from destruction of basal parts of the brain, became delinquent. Similar evidence comes from the observed effects of other lesions, notably in the temporal lobes and less often in the frontal lobes. The complexity of the problem is underlined by other recent experiments which have shown how the precise effect of a lesion may be dependent upon environmental factors, such as the social situation.

These and many more examples all indicate the way in which disorders of mental function are produced by damage to the brain. Moreover, there are no well-validated studies in neuropsychology that point to a mental storage of memories separated from their physical basis. And none of the disorders of mental function studied provides evidence of an independent mind able to compensate for difficulties created by the disorganization of the brain. It is not surprising, therefore, that experimental psychologists prefer to regard man as a unity, even though, in the course of investigating him and the biological basis of his behaviour, it may be necessary to analyse and investigate the same events from several different standpoints variously described as the mental and the physical, or the psychological and the physiological.

Another approach which we may regard as a 'dualism of aspect' approach, as contrasted with the 'dualism of stuff' approach, asserts that we should abandon any attempt to describe the structure of reality in a single unified set of categories. Some who take this approach point out, as we have done earlier in this book, that scientific concepts serve strictly limited functions in the fulfilment of specialized purposes. According to this view, therefore, freedom and determinism are concepts expressed in two different languages. There is the actor language used by the person who is freely choosing, and there is the spectator language used by the scientist observing the same set of events, namely the choice being made. The argument goes that both these languages are necessary to do full justice to the human experience of freedom. It is of interest that Neils Bohr, and some other distinguished physicists, speak of freedom and determinism as complementary descriptions of man, thus seemingly extending the idea of complementarity from the wave-particle models we discussed earlier, and using it in this context as a helpful analogy. This same approach has been taken by some psychologists, such as Carl Rogers, who, writing of the two elements of determinism and freedom in the psychological study of man has said,

> 'That these two important elements in our experience appear to be in contradiction has perhaps the same significance as the contradiction between the wave theory and the corpuscular theory of light, both of which can be shown to be true even though incompatible.'[3]

It should be noted that this approach of complementary language does not postulate two distinct kinds of 'stuff' that man is made of, and thus avoids the problems of the traditional dualist approach taken by Descartes. Rather it recognizes that to describe the varying aspects of human behaviour and human experience one may have to use a variety of concepts which cannot necessarily be fitted into a single neat system of ideas.

Another approach which closely scrutinizes the language being used has been taken by some linguistic analysts, who point out that, while the language of the scientist serves its purposes well and enables him to achieve his goals of prediction and control,

[3] C. Rogers and B. F. Skinner, *op. cit.*, p. 1057.

nevertheless there are other languages such as those of everyday affairs which are fruitful for other purposes. In this case the idea of complementary languages does not derive from an analogy with the Principle of Complementarity of physics, but from an analysis of the varying functions of language in human life. Such a view points out that, while determinism is a useful postulate within science, that does not mean that it is a universal rule about the world. It is one thing, they say, to be a useful rule of procedure for scientific inquiry, but quite another to go on to assert that such a rule expresses an intrinsic property of the created order.

Heisenberg indeterminacy and free will

We turn now to a consideration of other proposed solutions to our problem of how we should relate man's physical determinacy to his experience of freedom to choose, which make use of the Heisenberg Principle of Indeterminacy in physics. Several different versions of some kind of mind-brain dualism derived from, or dependent upon, this Principle have been adopted by some prominent neuro-physiologists. Not many years ago in a symposium of British scientists there seemed to be a wide measure of agreement that the neural activity of the brain somehow interacts with the private world of the mind.[4]

As an example of this sort of view which has been carefully developed, we may consider Eccles's suggestion that 'the mind-brain liaison occurs in the cortex'. According to this view the will of man can influence neural circuits without violating the physical laws because the energy involved in such influence is within the limits of the Heisenberg Uncertainty Principle. His suggestion is that there might be either an influence of the mind on individual quantum events whose effects can then be amplified through other parts of the cortex, or more probably that there could be a co-ordinated shifting of probabilities in many such events simultaneously. In either case the picture is of neural activity being changed by non-physical factors. MacKay[5] has made several comments on this approach. The first is that,

> 'The degree of physical indeterminacy allowed by Heisenberg's Principle becomes more and more negligible the bigger

[4] See P. Laslett, ed., *The Physical Basis of Mind* (Macmillan, 1950).
[5] D. M. MacKay, 'Brain and Will', *The Listener* (May 9th and 16th, 1957).

the objects that we are studying. Indeed it is only with the smallest objects of all—electrons for example—that this indeterminacy is really serious. A nerve cell may be a tiny object by everyday standards, but it is roughly a million million million times heavier than an electron; so that the chances of its suffering appreciably from Heisenberg indeterminacy are small indeed.'

Moreover, since there are about ten thousand million nerve cells in our brains, the chance that some one of these should be disturbed by a physically indeterminate event is correspondingly greater. And this leads to his second comment, which is that as far as we can see,

'The brain is not like a wireless set, in which a single valve failure is enough to upset the whole performance. The nerve cells in the brain seem to be organized on a principle of teamwork, often with hundreds or even thousands of cells working together on any one job—rather like the individual strands in a rope.'

This means that even if one of our brain cells is put out of action altogether, the chances are that it would make no significant difference, and indeed it has been computed that in the process of ageing, from about twenty years onwards, we all of us lose the use of several thousand nerve cells every day of our lives, but this makes only a very small difference to our normal functioning.

The third point made by MacKay is that the random variations in the brain due to the kind of disturbances that Heisenberg has discussed may turn out to be quite small compared with other sorts of random variations due to, for example, changes in the temperature of the brain tissue, random fluctuation in the blood supply and other kinds of disturbances reaching the brain from the outside world. To quote from a more recent statement by MacKay,[6]

'The sort of randomness required can be very easily, and I think more plausibly, put down to thermo-dynamic fluctuations in and around the neurons concerned, rather than to microphysical indeterminacy of the Heisenberg sort.'

When one considers these different sorts of unpredictable dis-

[6] D. M. MacKay, in *Brain and Conscious Experience*, pp. 466, 467.

turbance, one naturally wonders whether these could provide the kind of freedom in the brain's activity which we are looking for when we speak of freedom of choice implying responsible action. MacKay[7] thinks not.

> 'If an element of randomness came into the chain of control of my action, this would tend towards *excusing* me from responsibility for it rather than crediting me with responsibility for it.'

Such disturbances in fact seem to be more like the mental aberration which all of us experience from time to time, the kind of unaccountable lapse or idea that just comes into our mind, rather than what we mean by making a responsible decision. One final comment on this solution, perhaps a more far-reaching one from a long-term point of view, is to question whether Heisenberg indeterminacy is part of the warp and woof of the universe or rather simply an expression of our present ignorance in this field of science. We shall have more to say about this in a moment.

Another variant of this kind of solution, which makes use of Heisenberg's Indeterminacy Principle, is one which has been worked out in some detail by Pollard in his book *Chance and Providence*.[8] Pollard is himself a distinguished physicist and active Christian, and he has suggested that for God to be able to act in a universe of free responsible persons, chance must be an intrinsic property of that universe. Using as his starting-point the indeterminacy of the atomic world, Pollard sees this as the place where God's providential control can be exercised. Since providence is not overtly visible, its operation violates no natural law because God determines only which actual value among the naturally determined probabilities is to occur. There is perhaps a slight difference here between this view and Eccles's view, in that God can in this way influence events without in any sense acting as a physical force. We are not to imagine God as pushing electrons around, because even though in a particular unrepeatable event the outcome is different from what it would otherwise have been, due to God's providential control, yet we have not thereby violated the scientific description of it, because what it might have been can never be ascertained except as a set of alternatives.

---

[7] *Ibid.*, p. 464.   [8] W. G. Pollard, *Chance and Providence* (Scribner, 1958).

On this view, therefore, God does not have to apply any kind of extra natural spiritual force, nor does He intervene to manipulate natural probability patterns. Although common sense would suggest that anything which influences the position of an object would have to be some sort of physical force, this assumption rests on common sense and classical physics, rather than on modes of thought dependent upon quantum physics. On this view an electron in a probability distribution does not have a definite position, and so no force at all is required to influence the outcome. This is an ingenious and tenable hypothesis, once again provided that one accepts that Heisenberg indeterminacy is a built-in characteristic of the natural order, and not an expression of our present ignorance. We believe that there are good reasons for not adopting this position, since it means that it is vulnerable to further advances in natural science, which may yet indicate that unpredictability arises out of our present scientific ignorance rather than out of basic indeterminacy in creation. We must now seek to say briefly why we think this is so.

Indeterminacy and unpredictability

In the preceding paragraphs we have discussed this question of the use of indeterminacy in providing solutions to problems relating science and Christianity, with special reference to the problem of the freedom of man. Let us now for a moment extend the question a little wider and then return to this specific question of freedom of choice later on. The question now becomes, do we believe that for God to be able to act in the universe chance must be an intrinsic property of that universe? Or, more specifically, for God to act do the laws of nature at rock bottom have to be indeterminate with an indeterminacy of the kind expressed by Heisenberg's Principle of Indeterminacy? Or again, when, for example, God answers prayer, does this mean that God needs the loopholes which Heisenberg's indeterminacy would give him?

Clearly basic to our discussion of these questions are certain prior questions about the present position in quantum physics which we must discuss briefly in order to be able to go on to ask about any theological issues which seem to be at stake, depending upon the way in which we have understood the present views among physicists on indeterminacy. To understand this question we must introduce, in as simple terms as possible, some basic physical concepts for the benefit of those who are not professional physicists. In so doing we shall lean heavily upon the paper on *Physical Determinacy* prepared for the conference by Dobbs.

Dobbs reminded us that from the sixteenth to the twentieth centuries the accepted view was that the world resembled one huge machine which could be understood, at the atomic level, in terms of classical mechanics. On this mechanistic view the past and future of the entire universe is completely determined by the equations of motion of all the particles, together with their positions and velocities at any one moment. Classical theory in physics is thus completely deterministic. Moreover the conservation laws of classical physics still apply in quantum theory, where their revised form owing to Einstein is used for relativistic energies. And the laws of thermodynamics apply equally to a classical gas of molecules and a quantum gas of electrons in a metal. These classical laws are not abandoned in quantum theory; they are shown to be valid under a quite different set of initial assumptions.

Quantum theory began with Planck's hypothesis that radiant energy such as that emitted by a hot object can be emitted or absorbed only in integral multiples of a 'quantum' of energy, that is, to put it simply, in small chunks which are not further divisible. Dobbs wrote,

> 'Planck's hypothesis was at variance with the whole of classical physics, but at the same time it correctly explained the frequency spectrum of radiant energy and was also successful in its predictions of the variation of the thermal energy of solids with temperature. When Einstein found in 1905 that the same hypothesis explained the emission of electrons from a metal by ultra violet light, the quantum hypothesis was established and the classical idea of a continuous change in energy had to be abandoned. Many other experiments have since confirmed that energy changes occur discontinuously in discreet, indivisible quanta and not continuously.'

Further work by other scientists, notably De Broglie, soon made it clear that the classical electron must be replaced by the quantum mechanical 'wave packet' or short pulse of oscillations, so that the electron was no longer at a 'point', but was spread out over a distance in space and had a range of wave numbers in its wave packet. It was soon easily shown that a 'small' wave packet requires a wide range of wave numbers and *vice versa*. It was these relations, fully developed, which were to lead to the Uncertainty Principle of Heisenberg.

It can be shown from the basic postulates of quantum theory, and this has been confirmed experimentally, that certain pairs of variables such as those indicated are related to each other in a peculiar way. That is to say, the more accurately one of the quantities is known, the less accurately the other quantity is predictable. For example, the more accurately the position of an electron is measured in an experimental arrangement, the greater is the uncertainty in any prediction of its velocity. Much oversimplified, this is the famous Heisenberg Uncertainty Principle. The errors of measurement, therefore, that come in under these circumstances, are not the ordinary type of error that can be reduced by improving the sensitivity of the apparatus; they are, so it is asserted, inherent in the structure of matter.

In this way it became clear that the classical assumption of complete determinism is wrong. The classical concepts of momentum and position have to be refined to allow for the fact that they cannot exist simultaneously with perfectly defined values, for, as Dobbs put it :

> 'The complete determinism of classical theory arises from the fact that, once the initial positions and velocities of each particle in the universe are given, their subsequent behaviour is determined for all time by the forces acting on them as given by Newton's equations of motion. But now in quantum theory, Newton's laws cannot be applied in this way to a particle, since its momentum and position cannot be simultaneously defined with perfect accuracy. For example, if we wish to aim an electron at a spot, we must first locate it precisely and then give it that momentum which will cause it to move to the desired spot. Since the uncertainty principle shows that this cannot be done, the concept of causation through deterministic laws cannot apply. Causation can be described only by statistical laws. In a series of many observations in aiming an electron at a point by controlling its momentum a reproduceable pattern of hits will be obtained. Thus in quantum theory causality is a statistical trend not

precisely determined in each case. The explanation of events in quantum theory is thus different from the classical method of first describing space-time sequences of events, and then giving a causal account of the relationship between these events, since it is not possible to define the space-time and causal factors precisely at the same time.'

We are now getting near to seeing an answer to our basic question concerning the relation of indeterminacy to unpredictability, for, as Dobbs pointed out,

'It is sometimes suggested that the probability basis of quantum physics is a temporary difficulty only, such as occurs in the study of a critical state of a gas/liquid system by observing its thermodynamic variables. Here the thermodynamic parameters of pressure and temperature are statistical averages over the large number of molecules composing the system, and in rarefied gases, or near the critical point, they no longer obey an equation of state precisely, but exhibit large random fluctuations about their average values. To find the causal laws, we must use the concept of the positions and momenta of the molecules—dynamical variables which are "hidden" in thermodynamical theory. Perhaps there are similarly hidden variables which "really control" the exact time and place of transfer of a quantum, and we are just ignorant of them.'

This criticism of quantum theory was first made by Einstein and others in 1935, and has been repeated many times since.

To put the matter in another way, Einstein to the end of his life maintained the view that quantum mechanics is a discipline for representing our ignorance, not an account of the situation as it necessarily is. This viewpoint, discussed more recently by Bohm, faces us with a challenge, first to distinguish clearly and consistently between the unpredictability of a system and the determinacy of a system, and second, to raise the question of whether ultimately we can get down to a deterministic universe.

First, let us ask whether we have any grounds for saying that the Heisenberg Principle reflects indeterminacy as distinct from unpredictability. We may conceptualize an unpredictable but determinate system as one of which no complete future specification is possible to us, but of which a large number of identical replicas, released from identical initial conditions, would always be found later to be in the same state. Thus we may take an ensemble of systems and say that the system is unpredictable but still determinate, if when released from identical conditions all will be found later in the same state. Conversely an indeterminate system is a system in which, even if we had an ensemble of identical replicas, they would not if released from identical conditions be found later in the same state.

With these two definitions in mind the question now becomes, is the universe of the first kind, *i.e.* unpredictable but determinate, or of the second kind, indeterminate? If it is of the first kind then an ideal observer can predict its future state even though we cannot; if it is of the second kind then even an ideal observer knowing the initial conditions would not know what is going to come next. The challenge thrown out by Einstein, Bohm and others is whether in fact given time we can get beyond the Uncertainty Principle. If, as several past and present distinguished theoretical physicists think, it is only a matter of time before we do get beyond the Uncertainty Principle, then this means that to build one's Christian apologetic concerning human free will or any other aspect of Christian belief upon this principle may be quite a mistaken thing to do. As we have indicated in several connections already in this book, it is mistaken to tie one's theological beliefs to a particular scientific theory because it is widely held at a given time, since scientific theories by their very nature are subject to continuous change in the light of new evidence. If Einstein, Bohm and others are right, then the same will be true of Heisenberg's Uncertainty Principle, even though we cannot see how this could possibly be at the present time.

Having said this, it should be made clear that, while there are physicists like Einstein and Bohm who regard uncertainty as indicative of our human ignorance, there are at the same time others such as Neils Bohr who are convinced that uncertainty is not a product of our ignorance but a fundamental limitation on human knowledge, which permanently prevents us from knowing whether events in the atomic domain are determinate or not. Often those who write from this point of view subscribe to a positivist view of science. According to their view, probability functions are useful calculating tools for co-ordinating observations and they do not represent the real world. These kinds of interpretations are essentially agnostic, in the sense that they do not know whether the atom itself is determinate or indeterminate, and moreover they assert that we can never know.

There is yet another group who take the position taken by Heisenberg himself, that the Uncertainty Principle represents the fact that indeterminacy is an objective feature of nature itself and not a limitation of man's knowledge. What is our view? Clearly we are not competent to differentiate between these scientific views of three sets of experts who are not agreed among themselves, but our question is, from the point of view of Christian belief does it matter which view is correct?

As we have indicated above, our answer would be that it would seem improper and unnecessary to tie a particular aspect of one's Christian apologetic to a particular scientific theory, especially perhaps one that is so much under debate. But having said this, let us consider that view of the three outlined above which, on the face of it, presents the greatest challenge to belief in freedom of choice, and let us ask what would follow if the first group of scientists were correct, so that uncertainty was essentially an expression of our human ignorance. In other words we must ask the question, What if the universe turned out to be a fully determinate system after all? What implications would this have for problems such as those concerning human freedom of choice which we have been discussing earlier in this chapter? For example, if we made the assumption that the brain acts essentially as a physical system and that it therefore now becomes one which we must regard as essentially fully determinate, what implications does this have for our belief in human freedom?

If the solutions proposed by Eccles and Pollard are unsatisfactory because we feel that they are tied too tightly to Heisenberg's Indeterminacy Principle, the question remains, have we an alternative? Let us state our assumptions clearly. It has been argued by those who are highly skilled in computer technology and computer theory that the present barrier to imitating people artificially with machines is not at the level of computer theory and technology, but exists because as yet we find it extremely difficult to specify with sufficient precision the human behaviour which we wish to imitate. In other words, assuming that further psychological research enabled us to specify in detail the components of human behaviour that we are interested in simulating, then it is highly likely that the computer experts would be able to build a machine to carry out these specifications. It is clear then that the trend of present research provides no good reasons for doubting that the mechanisms of our brains are less mechanical than the mechanisms within computers. This is not to deny that in principle it is extremely difficult to produce such machines, but this is not our concern; our concern is with the principles underlying the working of the human brain. Given these two assumptions we can restate our problem as follows : if the brain were mechanical and if by this we mean that, given the initial conditions plus the equations embodying its methods of functioning plus the inputs to it at all times, we could deduce the future descriptions of it for all time, then what consequences would this have for our views of human freedom ?

Since we are going to set out the main features of an argument expounded in greater detail in several publications in recent years by MacKay, concerning the relationship between freedom of choice and the physical determinacy of the human brain, it is important that we make clear the use that we are making of the word 'free' in this context. We must distinguish carefully between two possible meanings of the word 'free'. If by 'free' we mean unpredictable by anyone, then clearly by definition the hypothesis we are considering assumes that a super-scientist who has a full knowledge of the present physical state of your brain-plus-environment, and of the equations upon which its future activity is based, can predict its future state, and in this sense your actions are not unpredictable by anyone. MacKay argues, however, that the kind of freedom we need for the idea of responsibility to have meaning and relevance is somewhat different.

In his recent Eddington Memorial Lecture, he writes,

> 'Let us now see how what we call a free choice appears in the light of our discussion. Suppose you have to decide at 7 p.m. whether to leave for the 7.15 p.m. train, or to wait for a later one. This means that just before 7 p.m. there are two possible descriptions of the future event at 7 p.m. : either (G) you decide to go, or (W) you decide to wait. Until 7 p.m. you contemplate G and W as *undetermined* alterna-

tives. At 7 p.m. you decided to go, thus making description G true and W false; and you act freely as far as you can tell. But next day a Determinist calls with a ciné film of data taken from your brain before 7 p.m., from which he can prove that the outcome was calculable in advance to be G. Does this evidence retrospectively refute your belief that your action was free?

'If "free" were defined to mean "unpredictable by anyone", then of course in that sense your belief would be falsified. I suggest, however, that this definition, though true perhaps of the "freedom" of *caprice,* begs too many questions to be adopted uncritically for the "freedom" of responsible action. Indeed on further analysis it seems to put the emphasis in quite the wrong place. An action might be rendered totally unpredictable by some random physical disturbance of your neural mechanism; but, as Eddington among others pointed out, this could well be held to diminish rather than enhance your responsibility for it. Conversely, some of your most responsible actions may be highly predictable by people who know you well, without any examination of your brain. Continuity in the mental processes leading up to a decision is not merely permissible but positively desirable if you are to be regarded as responsible. Ideally, indeed, most of us like to be able to confirm our responsible decisions by going over the ground more than once, to see whether we come to the same conclusion. If, however, before you made up your mind, there existed a determinate and unique specification of the outcome which could command the assent of everyone, including yourself, whether you knew it or not or liked it or not, then the case would be different. Here we would have to say that the outcome was not only predictable by others, but also *inevitable by you,* and you could not be held to have acted "freely".

'To call an action "free" in this sense is therefore to deny the existence of any determinate specification that is binding on (valid and definitive for) everyone, *including the agent,* before he makes up his mind. It is this kind of freedom that I suggest underlies human responsibility.'[9]

Taking this view, what we want to be able to say is that, if I am to be responsible for a choice, then no inescapable, determinative

[9] D. M. MacKay, *Freedom of Action in a Mechanistic Universe* (CUP, 1967), pp. 16, 17.

prediction must exist which is binding on me whether I know it or not, whether I believe it or not, and whether I like it or not. In other words a necessary condition for me to be free in this sense would be that as I confront the future there must not now exist for me any inescapable prediction to be drawn from the initial conditions plus the equations governing those conditions.

Let us imagine now a super-scientist who studies the state of my brain and who then, knowing the present conditions plus the equations that summarize the operating characteristics of my brain, makes a prediction concerning the decision which I am about to make in a given situation. Of course by definition if he keeps quiet about his prediction, and if he is in fact a super-scientist, he will be able to sit back and see his prediction fulfilled. An experiment of this kind, however, will prove nothing one way or the other about my ability to choose or my freedom; it will simply prove that the super-scientist really was super! In what sense, we may ask, is his prediction a true prediction? To put the question another way, What does he suggest that I would have been correct to believe at the time? If his prediction had the same inevitability as a forecast of an eclipse, for example, then it should be correct whether I see it or not, whether I believe it or not, and whether I like it or not.

Predictions about behaviour, on the other hand, turn out to be fundamentally different for the following reasons. According to the mechanistic determinist's own assumptions, whatever I believe is rigorously reflected in the state of my brain. It follows that no complete description of the state of my brain can exist which would be equally correct whether or not I believed it, since my believing it would (on the same assumptions) be reflecting a *change* in that state. The point is, that whatever prediction the super-scientist may write on paper, if it is to be valid for him it cannot be equally valid for me—I would in fact be *mistaken* to believe it, since my believing it would change the state of my brain in such a way that it no longer corresponded to the description of the brain state upon which the prediction was based. In fact, whatever else you may say about the prediction on the paper, for me it has no binding force: it has no inevitable claim on my assent, whether I know it or not, whether I believe it or not, and whether I like it or not. MacKay has put it like this:

'The key point is that if what a man believes affects correspondingly the state of his organizing system, no complete up-to-date account of that organizing system could be believed by him without being ipso facto rendered out of date.'[1]

He points out that this is merely a particular case of the general proposition that no information system can embody within it an up-to-date and detailed representation of itself, including that representation. This point was worked out in detail by Karl Popper some years ago when he showed that even with a determinate computing machine no such machine could produce a convergence onto a specification of its own future state which would still be valid if it was embodied into itself, because the actual embodying of that specification in its information system would make the specification out of date.

MacKay has described this dilemma in which the super-scientist finds himself by saying,

'In a very strict sense it [the description on the paper] is incredible—not only because you do not feel like believing it, but because any attempt on your part to believe it would make it out of date. We therefore have the logical paradox that a prediction based on what the man has written on the paper, although it may be valid for him as long as he keeps it to himself, is not "the real truth" in any universally binding and exclusive sense, because "the real truth" is something that anyone would be right to believe and wrong to disbelieve; but here is something which you would be wrong to believe—and which he knows you would be wrong to believe. If you believed it, you would make it out of date, and he would then be wrong to believe it too. For you it is logically indeterminate. . . . This, I think, goes very deep. It may not be obvious at first sight, but the point is that even the most accurate scientific predictions, relating to such states of the brain as we have been discussing, cannot be said to be universally "true", since they cannot be valid for the man whose brain it is.[2]

It is important to remember that this is not at all a question of our ignorance of brain processes. It is an inevitable corollary of

---

[1] *Brain and Conscious Experience,* p. 434.
[2] *Christianity in a Mechanistic Universe,* pp. 63, 64.

any theory, however deterministic, that assumes that our thinking is rigorously reflected in the workings of our brains, and MacKay continues, 'Even if brain functions were as mechanical as clockwork (which they are not), our choices would have this "built-in indeterminacy" which allows no advance prediction of them to be binding upon us.'[3]

To sum up we can say that MacKay, without espousing any particular scientific model of brain function, but merely starting from the mechanistic assumption of the determinist, has shown what does *not* follow from it. In MacKay's own words,[4]

'It will, I hope, be abundantly clear that in this whole discussion I have had no intention of urging a *belief* in mechanistic determinism, or even in computer models of the brain. My aim has rather been to loosen up a knotted skein of improperly linked questions in order that each may be disentangled and considered on its merits. I suggest in particular that the question whether all human brain activity has a mechanistic explanation is one we can peacefully leave open for future investigation, no matter how high a view we take of man's power of decision and its moral and religious significance. A complete mechanistic explanation of the brain would not eliminate our freedom, and those who urge mechanistic behaviourism so as to abolish moral and spiritual categories seem to be pursuing an illusion.'

He adds,[5]

'I am suggesting that fears of mechanistic explanations of brain function are groundless, not because we can be sure that the brain is not a machine, but because even if it were, the whole constellation of claims regarding our inner nature and significance and destiny expressed in our moral tradition and the Christian religion would remain unaffected. It is not people, but brains, that may, or may not, be machines. It is not brains, but people, that choose, freely or otherwise, and in so doing determine their eternal destiny.'

It should go without saying that if one does *not* begin with the mechanistic assumption of the determinist then there is no problem anyway concerning freedom of choice of a kind that seems ethically significant.

[3] *Ibid.*   [4] *Freedom of Action in a Mechanistic Universe*, pp. 36, 37.
[5] *Ibid.*, p. 38.

CHAPTER 7

RETROSPECT AND PROSPECT

IN this final chapter we shall briefly review the ground covered in detail in earlier chapters, with the twofold aims of learning from the past how to identify and avoid unnecessary and unreal conflicts between science and faith, and of working out some implications of a biblical view of science for the practice of science today. We have seen how from time to time tensions have developed between some scientists and some religious people which have broken out into open conflict expressed in accusations and counter-accusations. Not surprisingly such conflicts have always had a news value not given to those scientists, many of them eminent men, who have worked quietly away at their science and who at the same time have professed a deep religious faith. The net result has been that in the minds of many men and women who are not scientists there is now a tacit assumption that there has been a war between science and faith, that it is now over, that science is the victor, and that religion is now merely an archaic irrelevancy to be practised by a few people who 'happen to be made that way'.

We do not accept the view that science and faith are warring parties. Rather we have argued for the view that if there is a conflict it is not a conflict between science and faith, but between those who from time to time elevate human reason to a position where it becomes virtually an infallible guide, and those more empirically minded who are content to 'sit down humbly before the facts like a little child' and to be guided by those. We have sought to present evidence that there are good reasons for tracing a close connection between a scientific approach of rational empiricism and the Hebrew-Christian view of nature. In contrast, there is another view which supports an exaggerated assessment of human reason stemming from the rationalistic spirit which characterized some phases of Greek philosophical thought and which in various guises has recurred from time to time in the centuries since then. The Christian view of nature insists upon seeing man himself, including his mind and his capacity for rational thought as an integral part of nature. Such a view helps to overcome the temptation to ascribe to human intellectual achievements an exaggerated status verging at times on infallibility. Moreover we have argued that to elevate human reason to such a position has at times jeopardized the progress of science and could do so again. To sum up, we believe that a Christian approach to nature should be one of rational empiricism rather than of mysticism, existentialism or rationalism.

We have noted that we all build up thought-models, implicit or explicit, in order to produce for ourselves an integrated and coherent picture of the relation of God to His creation. We have seen how easy it is to build up models which distort a truly balanced picture in one way or another. Thus, on the one hand, one may overemphasize God's separateness from that which He has created or, on the other hand, one may overemphasize His immanence within the created order. Either way leads to a distortion of the truth. We have tried to illustrate this by examining some of the ways in which the concept of a law of nature has been used. It has emerged that, while on a Christian view laws of nature are descriptive, there are other views which, by regarding laws as prescriptive, either ignore or deny God's creative and sustaining activity. No longer, then, do they describe what is the case but purport to say what must be the case and what must have been the case. It is at this point that we feel it is vital to recall the important Christian doctrine that God not only creates but also sustains the whole universe moment by moment by His power. To give this doctrine full weight helps to make clear that to search for laws of nature does not exclude the possibility of events which have traditionally been labelled as miraculous.

Developing this line of thought further, we have seen how a careful reappraisal by scientists themselves of the nature of the scientific method and of the scientific enterprise has led, in recent years, to a much more realistic and modest evaluation of the scope of science. In the first place it has led to a renewed emphasis on the participation of the scientist as the knower, in that which he knows. This in turn has overcome the false dichotomy which had previously been built up between the objective knowledge provided by the scientific method and the subjective knowledge supposedly produced by all other ways of gathering knowledge. While not for one moment wishing to minimize the relative objectivity of scientific knowledge as compared with most other knowledge, it is now seen not as something essentially different in nature, but rather as knowledge in which the component of the knower differs from the other kinds of knowledge such as the aesthetic and religious.

As we have studied the thought-models used in science and in religion we have learnt an important lesson from science itself. The scientist who makes extensive use of thought-models is fully aware that such models are not to be identified with the reality which they seek to explain. We have wondered whether the same point is as fully appreciated and consistently adhered to in the use of religious thought-models. Indeed we have the impression that at times some Christians have improperly identified biblical images and thought-models with the spiritual reality which they are seeking to convey to us and portray to us. Failure to maintain this distinction has in the past at times resulted in improperly assigning particular meanings to those parts of the Bible which seem to make reference to the natural order. Moreover fully to grasp the fact that the Bible is not a scientific textbook helps us to see that we should not view scientific explanations of events as substitutes for or competitors with theological explanations.

But if they are not competitors or substitutes how then should they be related? One answer to this has been that any solution which we propose must do justice to the whole of our experience and knowledge. We emphasize this since we urge our non-Christian scientific colleagues to recognize that, just as their own attempts to integrate the whole of their knowledge aim at doing justice to all aspects of their experience, so likewise our attempts must fully take account of Christian experience, which is as much a part of our experience as our experience when we are taking measurements in our laboratories. When at times some Christian apologists have sought to fit God in the gaps of contemporary scientific knowledge, they have implicitly proposed a model of God's relation to nature which has ignored His moment-by-moment upholding power. Such a God-of-the-gaps model seems in danger of reappearing, no doubt in modern guise, as Christians seek to integrate the knowledge derived from the behavioural sciences with the pictures of man portrayed in the Bible.

More positively, we may note that two ways of relating science and faith constructively have received a considerable amount of attention in recent years. These two ways are quite similar to each other, but one of them will probably be more congenial to the experience and habitual ways of thinking of the scientist, while the other will appeal more to the non-scientist or the humanities man. The first uses as an analogy the experience of physicists which gave rise to the famous Principle of Complementarity. Essentially this asserts that in order to do justice to a set of events we may find it necessary to give more than one account of it, in terms of more than one conceptual framework or at different conceptual levels. In such cases we err if we try to oppose the accounts given within these two distinct yet necessary frameworks. Realizing that such an approach can easily become an excuse for always claiming to invoke another kind of explanation in order to justify the religious point of view, we have sought to emphasize the criteria which must be applied if this principle of logical complementarity is to be used properly and not abused.

The second approach referred to above makes use of the notion of transposition and was worked out in detail and popularized some years ago by C. S. Lewis. Lewis in his sermon 'Transposition',[6] begins by pointing out that the same sense-experiences can be interpreted in quite different ways on different occasions, depending upon the context in which they arise and the point of view from which they are interpreted. The subjective interpretation of the experience he labels 'emotion', and he points out that the correspondence between emotion and sensation is not a one-to-one correspondence. He goes on to say, 'And there never

[6] C. S. Lewis, 'Transposition', in *Transposition and other Addresses* (Bles, 1949), pp. 9-20.

could be a correspondence of that sort where the one system was really richer than the other. If the richer system is to be represented in the poorer at all, this can only be by giving each element in the poorer system more than one meaning. The transposition of the richer into the poorer must, so to speak, be algebraic, not arithmetical.'

He further illustrates his point when he says, 'If you are making a piano version of a piece originally scored for an orchestra, then the same piano notes which represent flutes in one passage must also represent violins in another', and he continues,

> 'The most familiar example of all is the art of drawing. The problem here is to represent a three dimensional world on a flat sheet of paper. The solution is perspective, and perspective means that we must give more than one value to a two dimensional shape. Thus in a drawing of a cube we use an acute angle to represent what is a right angle in the real world. But elsewhere an acute angle on the paper may represent what was already an acute angle in the real world : for example, the point of a spear or a gable of a house. The very same shape which you must draw to give the illusion of a straight road receding from the spectator is also the shape you draw for a dunce's cap. As with the lines so with the shading. Your brightest light in the picture is, in literal fact, only plain white paper; and this must do for the sun, or a lake in evening light, or snow, or human flesh.'[7]

Lewis later indicates that the important point is that what is happening in the lower medium can be understood only if we already have knowledge of the higher medium. Thus the piano version means one thing to the musician who knows the original orchestral score and another thing to the man who hears it simply as a piano piece. Likewise if we could imagine a creature who perceived only two dimensions and yet could somehow be aware of the lines as he crawled over them on the paper, we should easily see how impossible it would be for him to understand the three-dimensional aspects of the drawing of which we are aware. After a while as we pointed out that these lines represent a road and other things, he would soon begin to say, 'You keep on telling me of this other world and its unimaginable shapes which you

[7] *Ibid.*, p. 14.

call solid. But isn't it very suspicious that all the shapes which you offer me as images or reflections of the solid ones turn out on inspection to be simply the old two-dimensional shapes of my own world as I have always known it?'

Applying this approach to the relationship between what we claim to be spiritual life and the humdrum elements of our natural life (including our scientific activities), we soon see that if the spiritual life is richer, as we would claim it to be, then we are not surprised when the sceptic concludes that the so-called spiritual is really derived from the natural; this is exactly the sort of mistake which an observer who knew only the lower medium would be bound to make in every case of transposition. Spiritual truths, as the Bible reminds us, are spiritually discerned and the spiritual man judges all things and is judged by none. But this is where the problem becomes acute because the critic cannot be prevented from always inserting the words 'merely' or 'nothing but' to the experience which from our position of knowledge of the higher medium we interpret in a way which he interprets only from his position at the lower medium. In the most important sense, however, we should claim that he does not see all the facts until his own experience is opened to the encounter with God which alone can give him what he lacks. Thus even though in one sense he may properly continue to claim to have known all the facts so that there is nothing else to know, yet the meaning, the significance, of those facts is different from the spiritual point of view once such an encounter has taken place.

Perhaps the encounter of the two disciples on the Emmaus road is an illustration of such a change in understanding. No doubt as they walked with the risen Christ on the Emmaus road unaware of His true identity they were *factually* well acquainted with the prophecies in their Scriptures which were soon to take on a new meaning as He expounded them and showed their true significance. So it is that in one sense the scientific account of events, including scientific accounts of the behaviour of men themselves, leave nothing out; rather the Christian claim is that in these same events he sees a new meaning and significance interpreted from the higher spiritual medium.

Finally, let us try to enumerate the various attitudes towards science and scientific activity which we believe a truly biblical attitude towards creation positively encourages us to adopt. In the first place we enter into our labours as scientists with an attitude of freedom. This is that kind of freedom which is the birthright of all those who know God and have bound themselves to Him as the God of truth. It is well illustrated in the words of a seventeenth-century writer, Nathaniel Carpenter, who wrote, 'I am free, I am bound by nobody's word, except to those inspired by God; if I oppose these in the least degree, I beseech God to forgive me my audacity of judgment, as I have been moved not so much by longing for some opinion of my own as my love for the freedom of science.'[8]

The scientist who is a Christian can engage in his work enthusiastically and with an attitude of enjoyment, that of a son enjoying the inheritance given to him by his Father. Christians are sons of God, their heavenly Father, who created and sustains the natural order which He has given them to study, to enjoy, and to subdue. This means that scientific activities are properly regarded as one aspect of the fulfilment of the command of the Bible given to mankind to subdue the earth (Gn. 1:28). The Christian, however, being aware of the fallenness of creation, including his own reason, will always seek to submit that reason to the facts. He realizes that his reason is certainly not infallible and that he must constantly submit all his 'reasonable ideas' to the light of revelation and the facts elucidated by scientific endeavour. Furthermore, he will realize that there will be a constant temptation to submit facts to reason in a way which can easily lead to a distortion of the truth. Seeing himself now as a trustee of the natural order created by his Father, the Christian will seek to use the knowledge derived by all scientific endeavour in order that he may carry out more effectively the great commandment to love his neighbour as himself. In a word, he will seek to carry out his scientific endeavours efficiently, to increase his knowledge and control of the created order and to do this in such a way that he is able to use this knowledge to serve his neighbour more effectively.

As regards the status to be given to scientific theory, he will continually be aware of the constantly changing character of such

[8] Quoted by R. Hooykaas, in *Philosophia Libera: Christian Faith and The Freedom of Science.*

theory and thus will avoid elevating theories which at present are best able to handle the data to a position where they cease to be theories and so may become a hindrance to future scientific advance. At the same time, being thus aware of the constantly changing nature of scientific theory, he will eschew all attempts to make such theory the basis for ethical systems or moral codes, recognizing that these come from God by revelation.

From time to time, like anyone else, the Christian scientist will doubtless be depressed and discouraged as he faces difficulties in his scientific work. But he will take encouragement from the fact that, since he believes that God made man in His own image and placed him in this created world with the unique instruction to have dominion over all other creatures, he will therefore ultimately find that this faith engenders within him the confidence that man with the sensory and intellectual abilities endowed upon him, as he faces the phenomena which he perceives around him, will prove to be so adjusted to this that he will be able to acquire the knowledge which he needs in order to carry out his cultural charge.

Moreover, as he goes about his cultural charge the scientist who is a Christian and who knows that he is investigating his Father's world will do so with a freedom which he recognizes as a priceless treasure of the Christian gospel. He will know that this freedom positively encourages him to develop a free scientific discipline and to inquire into the world knowing that the Bible sets no bounds to the range of his inquiries. Such freedom, moreover, carries with it the gifts of an open mind which he knows must never be surrendered in the name of lesser ends, however laudable these may appear to be. But this open-mindedness must not be confused with empty-mindedness. It will be an open-mindedness combined with firm convictions, in contrast to a mere empty-mindedness characterized by an unreadiness to affirm anything. The freedom of such a truly open mind must moreover be a freedom at times ready and prepared to say simply, 'I do not know', especially in those instances where it is clear that, at least for the moment, there is no further duty to search for relevant data. Here more than anywhere else we must be ready to remain quietly open-minded rather than to submit to the temptation to plump for an unjustified conclusion, simply in order to be able to give the impression that we have the answer to every question.

With this assessment of the scientific enterprise in mind there should come a new sense of commitment in the activities of Christian scientists. A commitment which calls upon us not to neglect our talents, nor to pretend that we have no different talents than others who are in different walks of life. To do that would be to do despite to the God who has given us particular talents, and who, according to the teaching of Christ, will hold us solemnly responsible and accountable for the profitable use that we have made of them.

Finally, as in all that is truly Christian, our endeavours must be stamped with the hallmark of love. Love, not merely in the sense of general goodwill, but in the fuller sense of worship of the Creator and respect for His works. There must be no worship of the works, for that would be idolatry. Instead our worship will be expressed to the Creator in and through the way we set about investigating His works. Such love should be strong and adventurous; it should be infectious and temper every judgment that we make in our intellectual endeavours. It will not behave itself in an unseemly way, but will be so concerned for the well-being of the whole world and in particular of the church of Christ that it will seek to expose those not as yet equipped, either intellectually or by reason of limited education, to new ways of thinking and to new scientific knowledge at just the right time, in the right way, and above all in the right spirit. It will always remember that while all our efforts at ground-clearing may help our agnostic contemporaries to see that Christianity is possible, even plausible, nevertheless ultimately the knowledge of spiritual truth is not ours to give. Such knowledge comes only out of that ongoing personal transaction between each man and his Creator, which is the experience of every true Christian.

PARTICIPANTS IN THE INTERNATIONAL CONFERENCE OF SCIENCE AND FAITH AT OXFORD : JULY, 1965

PROFESSOR F. I. ANDERSEN
Professor of Old Testament, The Church Divinity School of the Pacific, Berkeley, USA.

PROFESSOR V. E. ANDERSON
Professor of Genetics, Dight Institute of Human Genetics, University of Minnesota, USA.

DR O. R. BARCLAY
Zoologist, Secretary of the Research Scientists' Christian Fellowship, London, England.

DR D. A. BOOTH
Lecturer in Experimental Psychology, University of Sussex, England.

PROFESSOR L. S. BOTERO
Facultad de Ingeniería Forestal, Universidad Distrital 'Francisco José de Caldas', Bogotá, Colombia.

PROFESSOR R. L. F. BOYD
Professor of Physics at University College, London, and Professor of Astronomy at the Royal Institution, London, England.

PROFESSOR R. H. BUBE
Professor of Physics, Dept. of Materials Science, Stanford University, USA.

DR S. BUCHHOLZ
Industrial chemist, Germany.

PROFESSOR J. O. BUSWELL, III
Professor of Anthropology, Wheaton College, USA.

PROFESSOR J. F. CASSEL
Professor of Zoology, North Dakota State University, USA.

PROFESSOR E. R. DOBBS
Professor of Physics, University of Lancaster, England.

PROFESSOR G. EWALD
Professor of Mathematics, Universität Mathematisches Institut, Mainz, West Germany.

PROFESSOR W. R. HEARN
Professor of Biochemistry, Iowa State University, USA.

MR P. HELM
Lecturer in Philosophy, University of Liverpool, England.

PROFESSOR R. HOOYKAAS
Professor of History of Science, Free University, Amsterdam, Holland.

DR J. T. HOUGHTON
Reader in Meteorology and Fellow of Jesus College, Oxford, England.

PROFESSOR M. A. JEEVES
Professor of Psychology, University of Adelaide, South Australia.

MR N. D. LEA
Engineer, General Engineering Co. Ltd, Toronto, Canada.

PROFESSOR T. H LEITH
Professor of Philosophy, York University, Ontario, Canada.

PROFESSOR D. M. MACKAY
Professor of Communication, Keele University, England.

DR H. MINATO
Lecturer in Chemistry, International Christian University, Tokyo, Japan.

PROFESSOR D. O. MOBERG
Professor of Sociology, Bethel College, Minnesota, USA.

PROFESSOR S. G. NILSSON
Professor of Physics, Lund Institute of Technology, Lund, Sweden.

DR J. C. POLKINGHORNE
Reader in Mathematical Physics and Fellow of Trinity College, Cambridge, England.

PROFESSOR C. H. PINNOCK
Professor of Theology, Southern Baptist Seminary, Louisiana, USA.

PROFESSOR B. RAMM
Professor of Theology, Seminary Knolls, Covina, California, USA.

PROFESSOR F. H. T. RHODES
Professor of Geology, University College of Swansea, Swansea, Wales.

PROFESSOR G. K. SCHWEITZER
Professor of Chemistry, The University of Tennessee, Tennessee, USA.

PROFESSOR G. J. SIZOO
Professor of Physics, Free University, Amsterdam, Holland.

MR S. SUTHERLAND
Lecturer in Philosophy of Religion, University College, Bangor, Wales.

PROFESSOR W. R. THORSON
Professor of Chemistry, Massachusetts Institute of Technology, USA.

PROFESSOR J. R. VAN DE FLIERT
Professor of Geology, Free University, Amsterdam, Holland.

PROFESSOR B. VOLKMANN
Professor of Mathematics, Mathematisches Institut A der Technischen Hochschule, Stuttgart, West Germany.

DR A. J. WEIR
Senior Lecturer in Mathematics, University of Sussex, England.

DR J. WHITE
Lecturer in Chemistry and Fellow of St John's College, Oxford, England.

PROFESSOR M. ZANDRINO
Professor of Biochemistry, Cordoba, Argentina.

INDEX